Grief to Grace

My story of tragedy, loss and recovery

By Lori Koos

Table of Contents

Introduction

During childhood we dream about what we would like to be when we grow up. "I want to grow up and be a nurse" or "I want to grow up and be a fireman" or "I want to grow up and be a cowboy" or "I want to grow up and be a teacher."

When I was a small child, I wanted to grow up to be a "model," "nurse," and a "mommy." This is the order I wanted my life from the time I can remember. Well, I grew up to be a mommy which was the best decision. The fulfillment I have received is tenfold to what money or a career ever could have provided me. My children are the most important thing to me in my life, next to God, of course.

The stories that you are about to read are factual events dealt to me in my life. When something unexpectedly bad happens, most people think they will not be able to endure the pain associated with that particular tragedy. I am here to tell you that you *can* deal with the pain. You *can* see the sunshine again. You *can* laugh again without feeling guilty. You *can* have as normal a life as you once did, if you allow it. It may not ever be exactly the way it was before, but with self work and lots of time you *learn* to move forward in a way that you can accept.

My first tragedy with Boone was my "wake up call." I was never, ever prepared for such agony. After his accident,

I always kept in the back of my mind other accidents that could happen but never expected any of them to occur.

When Jessica's tragedy came, my world completely stopped! I heard nothing for a long time and the world was silent to me! It was then that I realized that if I lived my life preparing for the bad things to happen, I won't be as shocked when they do happen. Is this crazy thinking? Yes! But that is how I lived for a long time, preparing myself for more tragedy because the pain hurt so badly that I wanted to be prepared for the worst.

The last tragedy was my school bus accident, and once again I wondered what was going on with my life. Would there ever be an end to pain?

I am sharing these stories with you because if there is even one person in this world who by reading them can gain any kind of peace during a bad situation, I'll know that my sufferings were not by chance.

My life was turned upside down three times. I used to wonder why God would allow such sorrow to enter into my life when I just wanted to be a good mother.

Through my sufferings I sought refuge with God. Yet, many times during my tribulations I did not like God. Many times I blamed God and was mad at Him because these things happened to me. But as I grew in my knowledge in Christ, I came to know that God does not want anything bad to happen to people either. Why then, you ask, would God allow such things to happen if it is not His will? I had the same question. I will answer by saying that if you read the New Testament, you will find reassuring answers as I have. I may never know why these things happened to me, but one day I will when I stand before Christ.

I now have the faith that accepts "all" things. I used to pray to God asking that He somehow change time for me, that He let me go back prior to these accidents. But it never happened. As I've said before, I may not like the things that have happened in my life, but I can't change them. Instead I have learned to deal with them. That is what this book is about, dealing with what life has given us, the good and the bad.

Don't take anything for granted. You could walk out your door today and your life could change in a flash with death, injury, an accident, cancer, family problems, etc... You don't know when tragedy will strike.

Keep an open mind as you read. My prayer is that you will be blessed knowing that God is real. God is alive in our hearts if we acknowledge Him. I would never allow myself to think of these stories as just "happenings" that came into my life with no significance of Christ's presence. I reached out to God for help and He heard my prayers!

Peace be with you as you read. God is truly good!

"The LORD gave and the LORD has taken away;
may the name of the LORD be praised."
Job 1:21

Boone's Story
A LIFE RESTORED

Dedication

To my son, Boone. This story is for you. You may never remember what happened to you on that tragic October morning in 1985, but I kept a diary of the events to let you know that God loves you and that He miraculously saved your life.

I love you with all of my heart, and I always will. Never, ever forget that you are loved by God and that He spared your life for a reason. Praise be to God!

Love,
Mom

Something Went Wrong

CHAPTER 1

Tuesday, October 29, 1985. It was a typical October morning, cool and crisp with beautifully colored autumn leaves covering the ground. I was seven months pregnant at the time. My daughter, Jessica, then age six, went to kindergarten in the mornings. I took advantage of her away time by scheduling a prenatal doctor's appointment for ten o'clock that morning. My son, Boone, would come with me to the appointment.

Boone was almost three years old. He attended my last doctor's appointment, at which he got to hear the baby's heartbeat. He was very excited to hear it again. When we arrived at the doctor's office, we were escorted to a room where the doctor greeted us and asked me how I was feeling. The doctor put his stethoscope to my belly and listened for the heartbeat. He once again put the earpiece into Boone's ears to let him hear the baby's heartbeat. Boone got so excited as he listened that he jumped up and down. After hearing the baby's heartbeat, Boone was convinced that he had a baby in his tummy also. There was no arguing with him that only girls have babies—he was going to have a baby, too!

The doctor gave me a perfect bill of health. We left the doctor's office glowing with the news that my pregnancy was on target. How could we have known that within thirty minutes a tragedy would come into our lives?

With Boone strapped into his car seat in the back of our 1976 GMC Jimmy Blazer, I headed for our home in the country. That afternoon, Jessica, Boone, and I were supposed to have lunch with Annette, a friend of mine that had a daughter Amanda, the same age as Jessica. As we drove closer to home, I couldn't remember if I was supposed to stop at the school and get Jessica or if Annette planned to pick her up when she went to get her daughter. I drove by Annette's house first. Her car wasn't there, so I assumed that she went to pick the girls up at school. I drove by the school, but I didn't see either her car or the girls there. I felt I needed to use a phone to make sure of our arrangements, and since I lived closest to the school I drove home to call Annette and make sure that she picked up both girls.

I drove into the west entrance of our semi-circle driveway, parked the Blazer, and told Boone to sit in his car seat. I told him I'd be right back. After I got out of the Blazer, I didn't shut my door.

The call took less than two minutes. I rushed back outside, jumped in the Blazer, and drove forward to go out the east entrance of the driveway. I didn't think to check on Boone in the back seat. He loved to go "bye-bye," so there was no reason to think he would have left his car seat. As I rounded the corner to get out of our driveway, mud puddles appeared. I felt a bump as I splashed through them. I thought I ran over one of our dogs or cats.

I looked in my rearview mirror and saw my son's maroon coat lying in a mud puddle. I thought to myself, *What in the world is Boone's coat doing in the mud puddle?* At that moment, I looked in the back seat and realized that he wasn't there. Boone had climbed out of the Blazer to play in the mud puddles. I just ran over my little boy.

My mind started to race. I slammed on the emergency brake and jumped out of the Blazer. I ran to my son and cried out, "Oh dear God, no, no! Oh my God, please let Boone be okay!"

As I kneeled down beside him, thoughts flashed through my mind: *He's not hurt. It's just a bad dream. He just fell down.* I turned him over and discovered that his face was covered with blood. He was not moving, and he appeared to not be breathing. I couldn't believe what I saw. I instantly picked him up. He was unconscious and bleeding. All I could do was pray to God.

"Please Lord Jesus, save my son. Don't let him die. Oh dear God, please save my son. Lord Jesus, Lord Jesus, please help me!"

I carefully ran into the house with my son in my arms. This was difficult for a pregnant woman to do. My first thought was to call Cindy, my sister-in-law, who was having a home decorating party at her house just up the road. I knew my mom and my sister were both there. But as I looked at Boone, he appeared lifeless. I quickly dialed 9-1-1.

A man answered my call, and I immediately said, "I need an ambulance. I just ran over my son's head. Please, oh my God, hurry!"

"What is your address?"

After giving the dispatcher my address I began to panic, thinking time was being wasted while my son lay so lifeless in my lap.

"Are you there? What is your name?"

"Yes, I'm here. Please hurry. Please help me! My name is Lori."

"Do not hang up the phone. I need to ask you several questions in order to help you. An ambulance is on the way and so is Life Flight. Lori, tell me if your son is breathing and conscious."

I put my face to Boone's mouth.

"Boone is not breathing and he is not conscious. Please dear God, please help me!"

"Lori, I need you to focus on what I am telling you. You are the only one there right now who can help your son. Listen carefully. Do you see any reason why your son is not breathing?"

As I looked at Boone I could see his mouth was full of blood clots.

"He has blood clots coming out of his mouth."

"Lori, you need to pull those blood clots out of your son's mouth."

"I can't do that! Oh God, help me."

"You need to do this now Lori. You can do this! Put your fingers in his mouth and pull them out. Once you've done this, let me know, and we will go to the next step. Your son's life depends on you doing this."

As I stuck my fingers in Boone's mouth and pulled the clots out I instantly could hear a gurgling noise as if he was trying to breathe. Blood started to flow more freely.

"Okay, I have pulled the clots out and I think he is trying to breathe."

"What color are his toes and fingers?"

"They are a light blue. Oh God, please help me." I knew that the blue color meant he was not getting any air. A different level of panic set in.

"Lori, I need you to calm down. You are doing a great job. Hang in there with me. The ambulance will be there any minute. You need to listen to me. I need you now to put your mouth over your son's mouth and nose at the same time and give him four little puffs of air."

I have never been trained in CPR, so I was quite hesitant, thinking I might screw-up and hurt my son more. But as I did what the dispatcher instructed me to do, I could tell that Boone was becoming a little more agitated.

"I think he is trying to breathe."

At that moment I heard the ambulance drive into our driveway.

"The ambulance is here! Oh God, thank you!"

"Lori, please do not hang up the phone yet. Go to the door and let them in and then let me know that the paramedics are helping your son."

"Okay."

I crawled on the floor with my son in my arms and unlocked the door. The paramedics instantly took Boone from my arms.

"They have my son. Thank you."

I disconnected from the dispatcher and called my sister-in-law's house. When Cindy answered the phone, I felt some reassurance in my mind, knowing that I was finally talking to my family.

"Cindy?"

"Yes, Lori?"

"Oh my God, Cindy, I just ran over Boone with the Blazer. I ran over his head!"

"We're on our way down," she answered.

As I paced around my living room, not really knowing what to do, a county police officer tried to calm me down and get some information on what exactly happened. I kept asking the officer if my son would be okay. I needed some reassurance.

During this chaotic scene, I remembered a Bible verse that I memorized a while back:

No temptation has seized you except what is common to man. And God is faithful; he will not let you be tempted beyond what you can bear. But when you are tempted, he will also provide a way out so that you can stand up under it.
I Corinthians 10:13

I hung on to the hope that God wouldn't let Boone die because I wouldn't have been able to bear knowing that I was the one who ran over him. If Boone suffered irreversible damage, I would want to die myself. That reassuring verse was the hope that I hung on to during Boone's ordeal.

The paramedics cut Boone's clothes off and took him out into the ambulance to work on him. It was then that my mom, sister, and sister-in-law drove in our driveway. I wanted to be comforted by them so much, yet I was afraid of what they would think of me for running over my child. My sister, Patti, grabbed my shoulders and said, "Oh my God, Lori, this can't be true!" Then both my mom and Cindy started questioning me about what happened.

The paramedics didn't want us around the ambulance with our questions. They had work to do. A police officer intervened and asked us to go in the house so he could get my statement. While inside, I kept waiting for someone to yell at me for not noticing that Boone was missing from his car seat. But no one ever did. We all knew it was just a horrible, horrible accident.

As we waited inside the house, the sound of a helicopter came roaring overhead. We all went back outside and watched as a Life Flight helicopter landed in our field. The paramedics quickly transported Boone into the helicopter to take him to a hospital in Portland, nearly an hour's drive from my house. When the paramedics were carrying Boone to the helicopter, he started to cry. They told me this was a good sign. I wanted to ride with Boone, but I couldn't because I was pregnant. It was against their policy.

The helicopter took off, and my family and I went back into the house. I wanted to just get in a car and go, but we needed to make a few quick phone calls before driving to the hospital. I needed desperately to contact Boone's dad, Randy, who was out driving a log truck near home that day. We called the dispatcher of the logging company and asked him to tell Randy there was an emergency at home and that he was to go directly to the hospital in Portland. I didn't want someone telling him what happened over the CB radio for fear that he would drive like a maniac to reach us, but I didn't have a choice.

My father and my brother, Mike, were also out of the immediate area. They had left a few days prior to the accident to go elk hunting with a friend up in the mountains of Walla Walla, Washington. They would be there for a couple weeks. Fortunately, my brother had a cell phone in his truck, so he periodically called to let his wife know how things were going.

Mike had just called Cindy right after I called her house. She told Mike to call back in half an hour, after she knew more about what happened. When Mike called back, we told him which hospital Boone was being flown to, but that we didn't know what his condition was yet. We told him to call the hospital in about ninety minutes. We hoped to know something about Boone's condition by then.

Lastly, I called Annette who had picked up Jessica from school. I told her what happened, and she graciously offered to watch Jessica until we knew more about the situation.

After my mom helped wash the blood off my hands, arms, and face, I changed shirts and grabbed two of Boone's stuffed animals. We finally set off for the hospital.

I left our Blazer in the driveway, just as it was when the accident took place. I left the keys inside the truck so that Randy would have something to drive to the hospital. As we were walking out to Cindy's car, I looked back to where I had seen Boone lying in the mud puddle. One little shoe lay all alone in the mud puddle. I walked over to retrieve it and burst into tears.

We got into Cindy's car and took off to the hospital. As we headed out of town, the reality of the situation hit me. We were going to the hospital to see my son, Boone, whom I had just run over with my vehicle. I kept replaying in my mind the image of Boone's face when I first turned him over in the mud puddle. I kept grabbing my own face, as if I could stop the pain by doing so.

"Dear God, please let Boone be okay, please God," I prayed.

Patti then led us all in prayer as Cindy kept driving. Once again, 1 Corinthians 10:13 came to my mind. God knew how much I could bear.

After we got on the highway, we got stuck behind a slow-moving truck for about fifteen miles. I'm sure it was God telling us to slow down and have faith in Him. Of course, when emotions are involved, we don't always hear God the best.

My mind was going crazy as we plodded along. I wanted to be with my son, and I wanted to know how he was doing. I kept picturing Boone in my rearview mirror, lying in the mud puddle.

"Oh God, please let him be okay, please God," was my constant prayer.

When we finally made it to the hospital, we followed the signs to the emergency room, although we had no idea where Boone would be. Hospital personnel had been waiting for us inside. They took us upstairs to a waiting room and told us that someone would come to give us news on Boone's condition.

Through all of this waiting, I felt so helpless. I had no idea what my son's condition was, and I couldn't do anything to help. Boone was in someone else's care. All I could do was pray for him.

When a doctor finally came out to speak with us, his report was not what we wanted to hear. The hospital hadn't taken X-rays yet. The doctor informed us that it was possible Boone's nose was detached, his cheek bones were crushed, his jaw was broken, and his skull was fractured.

Oh dear God, I thought, I've damaged him beyond repair!

I still hadn't lost hope, though. The only thing I was concerned about was whether or not Boone was going to live or die. *"Dear God," I prayed, "I will take Boone any way. Just give him back to me. I'll accept him in a wheel chair, but please, please, let him have a normal brain. Don't let him be trapped in a world of his own."*

After the doctor left, we looked without expression at each other. My family kept reassuring me that Boone would be fine. I had to believe them. I wanted so badly just to let myself go, to scream, cry, or throw something, but I couldn't. I knew I had to remain as calm as possible for the sake of the baby I was carrying.

We were soon led to the intensive care unit for pediatrics, where Boone was being treated. We were told once again to wait in the waiting area. Another doctor would be with us soon. About fifteen minutes later, a different doctor came out to the waiting room and informed us that Boone was in a stable but critical condition. It would be a while before I could see him or before they could tell us of the severity of his injuries.

It was very reassuring to hear that Boone was alive and stabilized. I thanked God for the report.

With another wait ahead of us, I decided to get something to eat. I wasn't hungry at all, but I knew I needed some sort of nourishment for the baby inside of me. My mother and I made a quick trip to the cafeteria. On our way back, we spotted Randy walking toward the elevator. I ran right for him. He put his arms around me, and I started to sob.

"My God, Randy, I ran over our son. I ran over his head. Do you hate me?"

"Of course I don't hate you."

From that moment at the elevator, all the way through Boone's ordeal, Randy was one hundred percent supportive of me.

Randy, my mother, and I went back up to the ICU and waited for the doctor. It had been hours since the accident, and I wanted to see my son. When the nurse came out to tell Randy and me that we could finally see Boone, I walked as fast as my legs could carry me through the double doors that led into the pediatric ICU.

Watching and Waiting

CHAPTER 2

W hen Randy and I walked into Boone's room, he was in a private, single room, lying in a crib with both guardrails pulled all the way up. Two nurses stood by, tending to my little boy. An oxygen tent covered his body, and his arms and legs were tied down so that he couldn't pull the tubes and monitors off when he woke up. Boone was sedated and sleeping.

I couldn't stand the sight of my son hooked up to all sorts of machines, tubes, and IVs. My emotions took over my body, and I felt like I was about to faint. The nurses told me to sit down in a nearby rocking chair to regain my strength for another look.

Boone looked better than the last time I had seen him, when he was bloody and not moving. He looked peaceful as he lay still in the crib. His right eye had swollen to about the size of a golf ball. Over the same eye a cut had been stitched closed. The rest of his body had some scratches, one on his left leg and a big one on his head.

I sat for a few minutes in the rocking chair and wondered *What do I do? What am I supposed to do?* As I looked around the room, it seemed like business as usual for the nurses and doctors. They all seemed so calm, knowing exactly what to do. Then there was my husband and me, weak, facing at a situation no person hopes they will ever have to face.

X-rays were taken before we were allowed to see Boone, but the results hadn't come back yet. We asked the nurses all sorts of questions as we waited for the report: "What is this machine for?" and "What does that machine determine?" Watching the machines do their work helped us pass the time, but not always in a productive way. Whenever Boone's temperature rose or his breathing rate changed for the worse, we panicked.

As the wait for the X-ray results continued, Randy and I went back to the lobby to pass the time. A nurse came out to assure us that Boone was getting the absolute best of care. She told us that at the same time Boone was being flown to the hospital, surgeons were finishing up a brain tumor operation on a little girl in the same ICU ward. An experienced neurosurgeon and the team of other doctor's who operated on this little girl were all there when Boone was brought in. We knew that this was no coincidence. God had those doctors there at that time for Boone, also.

After nearly two hours had passed, Randy realized that he left the Blazer downstairs in the emergency driveway with the keys in the ignition and the motor still running. We actually laughed at the situation. Because of the part of town we were in, we half expected the Blazer to be stolen when we went to check on it. Fortunately, someone in our family had already moved it for us.

When we came back to Boone's room, the neurosurgeon (the "head doctor") was waiting for us with the results of the X-rays. Boone had a skull fracture. The doctor explained that with a skull fracture, it is quite easy for a patient to experience some spinal fluid discharge, from which one can develop spinal meningitis. I knew what spinal meningitis was, and I knew it could be fatal. I started to panic again.

Boone's X-rays also showed a bruise on the back of his cerebellum. This was where the most damage was done. The neurosurgeon told us how the cerebellum is a specialized part of the brain, about the size of an orange, tucked under the cerebrum at the back of the head. It deals with a person's equilibrium and coordination of movements.

The doctor told us that Boone's cerebrum seemed to be fine, based on the results of an electroencephalogram (EEG) test that monitors brain waves. Boone's mind was not going to be affected by the accident. This was great news. God truly answered my earlier prayers for no damage to Boone's mind.

Next, we were told that Boone might be suffering from a broken jaw. If that was the case, the doctors would have to wire his jaw closed. We wouldn't know if that was necessary until the next morning, when a "face doctor" was consulted. (Because so many doctors were involved with Boone's recovery, I found myself nicknaming them according to their specialties: the "head doctor," "the eye doctor," "the tummy doctor," and so on.)

After being told that we would have to wait until the next day for any more news, we walked back out to the lobby to update the rest of the family.

On our way out of ICU I looked at Randy and said, "I can't believe this is happening. Our day started out so normal."

"Boone is going to be Okay Lori."

"I can't believe I ran over him. At least his brain is going to be Okay. I can deal with the other issues as long as I know Boone is aware of his surroundings and that he knows who we are."

***

We found out that Mike's earlier call to Cindy was divinely timed. He, his friend, and my father were in a

27

remote part of the mountains, inaccessible by vehicle. They had parked Mike's truck where they could and then traveled by horse to their camp. That day, Mike and his friend decided to take their horses to visit another camp. Along the way, Mike stopped at his truck to grab his cell phone and call home. Cindy wasn't expecting to hear from him for at least another couple days.

My dad had stayed back at the camp to rest, so he had no clue at first what happened. During the chaos, a friend of my father's who owned an airplane flew over the area where we thought my dad was camping. As he flew overhead, he blanketed the area with fliers instructing my father to call home ASAP. I don't think my dad ever found one of those fliers. He saw the airplane flying overhead and wondered what was going on, but it was Mike's call home that made the difference. Had he not made that call, it would have been days before Mike and my dad knew what happened. This was another miracle to us.

Looking back, I consider it another miracle that Randy was around. Ever since Randy and I had been married, he had always gone elk hunting with Mike and my dad. But this particular year, he made arrangements with a friend of his from high school to go elk hunting in Idaho. He had already gone on his hunting trip for the year, so he passed on going with Dad and Mike. I believe God worked it out so that Randy was close to home that day.

My dad finally called the hospital that evening. My mom tried to talk him out of coming down that night. After all, it was about a six-hour drive from Wall Walla. He wouldn't get to the hospital until about three in the morning, and my dad was known for falling asleep at the wheel. But it didn't matter. I wanted my daddy there at the hospital with me so badly. There is something about a daughter having her father with her in a difficult situation that brings her such peace. I wanted my daddy to tell me that everything would be fine.

As soon as he got on the phone with me and asked if I'd like for him to be there, there was no stopping him from coming. I said yes, and he was on his way. I knew he would not have slept that night anyway.

***

That first night was incredibly long. There were so many things I had to think of. Who would feed the horses at home? Who would clean the blood in the house from where I was holding Boone in my lap? Who would get our mail? And most importantly, who would take care of Jessica?

As I sat and worried, my mom tried to assure me that everything would be fine. My sister said she would pick up Jessica the next morning and take care of her. Jessi, as we called her, was still at my friend's house. She knew that Boone had been in an accident, but she didn't know details. Randy and I called her that night and explained to her what happened. At first, she had a funny mental picture of Boone's head being flattened like a pancake. It was a natural image for a cartoon-loving six-year-old to form in her mind. After all, that's what the Road Runner and the Coyote looked like whenever they got run over.

A friend dropped by the hospital to bring us an "emergency basket" filled with toothbrushes, combs, toothpaste, clean clothes, make-up, and other toiletries. We considered it a major blessing, since we didn't want to leave the hospital.

Dad arrived at the hospital around three in the morning, as predicted. That night, Randy, Mom, Dad, and I slept at the hospital in the lobby just outside the doors to the pediatric ICU. The staff gave us blankets and pillows. We felt a little timid about camping out in the lobby, but the nurse said that it was common to see in hospitals. In the ICU ward, people aren't permitted to sleep on cots as they are in the other parts of the hospital. We had to make due with what was available.

The sun finally started to come up, and the first day was behind us. It was a new day, and we wanted to be in good spirits for Boone.

Around seven o'clock that morning, the doctors started making their rounds. When the doctors were in the room or the nurses were changing shifts, there was a two-hour wait during which we weren't allowed in the ICU. It was always kind of nerve-racking during those times. We knew the doctors were discussing Boone's case with those taking the next shift, and we also wanted to be informed of his progress. During those times, we usually went to the cafeteria to grab a bite to eat.

That morning we ate breakfast and then stopped in the chapel to pray. It was such a quiet, peaceful room. We were able to sit and concentrate on our thoughts. My mom, dad, husband, and I all prayed. We prayed that God would heal Boone successfully and that this incident would somehow bring glory to God.

As we were leaving the chapel, I noticed a plaque on the wall that read GOD IS WITH US. Chills ran through my body as I read those words. I felt hope at that moment.

We returned upstairs to visit Boone. He looked so little in his crib. We tried once again to analyze the machines. Was he breathing better? Was his temperature normal? Were things going better? The nurses said that Boone had a peaceful night's rest and had stabilized very well.

I uttered thanks to God as I pulled up a chair and sat next to Boone. I wanted to spend time with him, to be there for him, but it was hard to sit there and just watch him sleep. He still hadn't awakened since his accident. As I watched Boone, I couldn't help touching my hand to the right side of my face. That was the side of Boone's face that was most injured.

I knew the Lord was working in this situation. We felt God's presence and power continually, and as Christians we never second-guessed where our strength came from.

Lots of people were praying for Boone. We were told that he was being prayed for by the 700 Club, a televised Christian program that aired in the eastern states. This was an uplifting report.

Many ministers from all different types of churches came to pray with us. It was overwhelming. I knew God was in control, and I knew God was allowing Boone to live.

Boone had done so well during the night that I knew it could only get better. His breathing during that second day kept getting stronger and stronger. He was able to breathe more on his own, and the nurses were able to turn down the oxygen rate on the machine.

Visitors poured in and out all day. This encouraged me, but it was difficult for Randy. Randy's parents died when he was a small boy, so he was raised in a foster home until he graduated from high school. He basically grew up on his own. He wasn't at all fond of large gatherings of people. In this situation, he felt people were showing up just to be nosey. He hated being asked questions. He didn't want to inform others that he didn't really know the intricate details of our son's life. Randy had to learn that people were there to support us, not to find some juicy gossip. I had to assure him that our friends were there because they truly cared about Boone and us.

Boone was sedated all that day, but his breathing continued to get better. The nurse told us the doctor's were considering taking the breathing tube out of his mouth if he continued to do well.

More visitors started to arrive as evening set in. I enjoyed the support, but I felt like I needed to entertain them somehow. After all, most of them came from an hour away. All I really wanted to do was be in Boone's room. I felt Boone needed to sense my presence, even though he was still sedated and asleep. I stopped worrying about the visitors and just did what I had to for Boone, for myself, and for my unborn baby. If I was tired, I slept. If I needed a shower, I took one. If I was hungry, I ate. It didn't matter who was there.

The sun started to rise on day three. We folded all our blankets and moved our pillows off into a corner of the lobby where we had been camping. Boone slept well throughout the night. After checking up on him, I walked down to the maternity ward for a very long, hot shower. The maternity staff had been kind enough to let me shower in their ward during our campout time in the lobby. I turned the shower into my personal prayer chapel. Whenever I was in the shower, I was by myself and relaxed, so I would just talk with God. He was the only one who knew how I was truly feeling. He was the only one who knew how Boone was doing and what was going to happen. As I talked to God during my shower times, I always had a peaceful feeling deep in my heart.

Boone continued to do well on his third day. It was Halloween, which was a hard day for me because Boone had been looking forward to trick-or-treating for the past month. We had already purchased his costume weeks in advance. It was a scary monster mask with blue curly hair hanging down from the top of the mask. We were going to dress Boone in some raggedy, ripped clothes to top it off. He had been wearing the mask around home daily preparing to scare his grandpa.

It was also a big day for Jessi. She had a big Halloween party at school, and she was very excited about it. It was a tradition each year for my sister and me to take the kids to friends' and relatives' houses for trick-or-treating. I toyed with the idea of going home that night and taking Jessi trick-or-treating. I thought it would be nice for me to go home and get a good night's sleep in my own bed.

Some sort of community organization delivered balloons and treats to the hospital's pediatric ward. Boone received a pumpkin-shaped helium balloon that the nurses tied to the end of his bed.

As I watched Boone, he was beginning to become a little more active, moving an arm or leg. One time he started to cry a little as he arched his back. When he realized he couldn't move (he was still tied down by his hands), he went back to his sleep. The doctor told us this was a self-induced coma. That was the first movement I had seen in three days. The nurses had informed us that during his spit baths there had been some movement, but I had never seen it. The nurses still discussed taking the breathing tube from his mouth that day. He was breathing much better.

All morning long and into the early afternoon I contemplated whether or not to go home that night. I really wanted to spend some time with Jessica. I wanted things as normal as they could be for her. Around three o'clock that afternoon, I finally made the decision to go home and take her trick-or-treating. Randy would stay at the hospital to be with Boone.

I walked outside the hospital for the first time in three days. The fresh air filled my lungs to capacity, and I felt much more alive. I was afraid to drive on my own still, so my mom drove me home.

Mom dropped me off at my house before she went into town to run some errands. I wasn't prepared for the support I would find there. We had received an abundance of cards and letters in the mail. One in particular still impacts me today.

The letter was from a man who was in jail on a traffic violation. He read about Boone's accident in the paper and wrote to tell me how he had a similar accident happen to him. He wanted me to know that he understood how I felt, and he encouraged me not to put the blame on myself. He said that children will be children, and they are hard to watch all the time.

I was very touched by that man's word. He was a total stranger, and judging by the fact that he was in jail, he was no doubt having some major problems of his own. Yet, in the midst of his problems, he wrote to comfort me. It's an act of compassion that I will never forget.

Patti brought Jessi over to our house so I could spend time alone with her before going trick-or-treating. I explained to her what was going on with her brother and what his injuries were. Jessica had such deep compassion for Boone. She was like a second mommy to him. She wanted to be with Boone at the hospital, so I told her that the next day someone would bring her in to see him. We hugged each other lots during our alone time, and then we prepared her costume for the night's festivities.

Back in My Arms

CHAPTER 3

That night Jessi and I had a wonderful time trick-or-treating together. Afterward, we stayed the night at Mom and Dad's house. Before we went to bed, I called Randy at the hospital to see how Boone was. He said everything was fine. In fact, the staff had taken the tubes out of Boone's mouth and nose. Boone was breathing on his own. This was yet another answer to prayer.

I tried to sleep that night, but my thoughts were with Boone constantly. At three in the morning I got up and called the ICU to see if anything had changed. The staff assured me that Boone was fine. He was sleeping peacefully. I tried my best to do the same, but tossed and turned all night.

Early in the morning I gave up on a good night's sleep. I got out of bed, got dressed, and tried to move things along so we could return to the hospital as soon as possible. After breakfast, Mom and I dropped Jessica off at school and then headed straight to Portland. When we got to the hospital, Randy met us at the entrance with a big smile on his face.

"Boone talked," he said. "He asked, 'Where's Mama?'"

I started to cry. I knew I was going to get my little boy back.

Randy told us that Boone also looked at him and bluntly said, "Dad, I want out." Boone was aware of his surroundings. He knew what was going on, and he wanted to no longer be stuck in his crib.

"Oh thank you, God! Thank you so much," I prayed.

Boone was asleep when I got to his room. He looked so good without the tubes in his nose and throat.

It was difficult for me to sit and watch him be so still. Boone was a typically active little boy. He never stayed put for more than one minute. Most of the pictures I have of Boone show him doing something active—playing in the mud, digging through cow pies in the barn, throwing cats in the swimming pool, spray-painting the trees, dumping baking soda all over the kitchen floor. He was always doing something.

I wanted to hear Boone talk. I wanted to hear the sound of his little voice saying, "Mama," once again. He was my little mama's boy, and I missed him. He loved his daddy, but Mama was his buddy.

Randy, Mom, Dad, and I had lunch in the cafeteria. A cousin of mine came by to visit during that time. The nurses let her in to see Boone while the rest of us ate. When she found us downstairs, she told me the good news that Boone was again asking for Mama.

I rushed back upstairs and into his room. There he was, looking at me.

"Hi, honey. I love you!" I said.

"You love *me*?" he asked.

My heart melted as I heard his voice. Boone knew who I was. He called for me by name.

"I love you, Mama," he said.

My whole being filled up with joy.

***

The "head doctor" examined Boone and discovered some leakage of spinal fluid from his nose. The doctor ordered a spinal tap to make sure there wasn't any meningitis or other sort of bacterial invasion elsewhere in Boone's body that would have caused the leakage. When the doctor drew the spinal fluid from Boone's body, it had a pinkish tint. Some blood was in the fluid. We were told not to panic, that it was a typical occurrence for the type of injury. Regardless, this was our first real letdown during Boone's time at the hospital.

We would have to wait seventy-two hours for the test results. It seemed like such a long time to us. We immediately began to pray that Boone would have no impurities in his spinal fluid.

The doctor told us that it was very important for no one with a cold or any type of sickness to get near Boone during this time. Randy and I became very strict about who could see our son. We let no one, not even family, see him. Randy, myself, the doctors, and the nurses were the only ones allowed in the room.

Later that day, a small boy was admitted to the pediatric ICU. We asked one of the nurses what was wrong with that particular child. She told us he might have spinal meningitis. Randy and I looked at each other and felt panic set in. We didn't want this boy anywhere near Boone. Fortunately, the boy just had some sort of intestinal infection. Needless to say, we were relieved.

Visitors came in the evenings. It was a time I looked forward to. I was still feeling all the guilt for Boone's accident. When visitors spoke to me, they told me that I shouldn't take it personally; it was just a terrible accident. Hearing this was very healing for me.

Randy's sisters were always the ones we could count on for evening visits. His oldest sister, Blanch, was a night owl. She usually came after nine o'clock at night. This was great for us. Most of the guests were usually gone by that time, so we could sit and visit one-on-one. Randy's other sister,

Donna, a welder, worked in Portland on a swing shift. She often visited after work, even after midnight sometimes. That was fine, too. We usually didn't sleep much anyway. All in all, our support group among family and friends was great.

Randy and I quickly developed a new morning routine. We would talk about the day before, and then set goals for the new day. On the day Boone's spinal tap results were due back, our goal was to talk with Boone and let him know we were there at all times for him. He was asleep for our entire morning visit, so we didn't get to talk with him. During the nurses' shift change, we took turns showering. One of us always stayed in the lobby, just in case a doctor needed to contact us.

After our showers and quick breakfast, we hurried back to the ICU to see the doctors before they left. No bad news was reported, but they were still monitoring Boone closely. He was still listed in critical condition. When we walked into Boone's room, he was resting. I still couldn't believe all that was going on. Things like this just didn't happen to people I know. I'd read about horrible accidents in the newspapers, but never to anyone I had known.

As we watched Boone sleep, my thoughts wandered. *Would he be normal? Would he be able to think? Would he be able to come out of all this?*

The nurse walked into the room and asked if I'd like to hold Boone for a while.

"Can I really?" I asked.

"Sure. He needs to feel your security and love." she said.

I was so excited. It was like I was going to hold a newborn baby for the first time.

I sat in a rocking chair, and the nurse propped pillows all around my arms. As she scooped up Boone, all his tubes and IVs dangled around him. I thought it wouldn't work out, but the nurse was very patient as she fixed all the tubes and laid my little Boone in my arms. I thanked God once again for sparing my son.

As I felt Boone's flesh in my arms, I took his little hands and held them. I fixed his hair and kissed his cold little cheeks.

"I'm here son. I love you," I said. "Mama is here. It's going to be okay."

Randy had a gleam in his eyes and a bright smile as he watched. This was the first close contact I had with Boone since I had carried him into our house to call 9-1-1. I had the sudden feeling that everything was going to be fine.

I held Boone for about twenty minutes before I started to cramp up. Being pregnant didn't help my lap any. The nurse once again picked Boone up and laid him back in his crib. He was asleep the whole time.

I couldn't wait to tell the family that I was able to hold Boone. It was such a good day for us.

***

Between four and five in the afternoon, the doctors started to make their rounds before going home. We were informed that Boone's test results were negative for spinal meningitis. Boone was successfully progressing at a slow rate. After all he'd gone through there was absolutely no need for any surgery. It was one miraculous report after another.

The next morning, after our showers and breakfast, we were able to see the doctors again. They had removed Boone's oxygen tent. He looked so much better lying there with no tent over him. His little body was much warmer with the oxygen tent off. He just looked great.

Boone was able to talk a little better now. As he looked up at us, he noticed the balloon that had a pumpkin face on it.

"Punkin', Mama," he said.

"Yes, that's a pumpkin, honey," I replied.

Before Boone's accident, Jessi went to the pumpkin patch with her kindergarten class. Boone was hypnotized by the pumpkin she brought home. Randy and I decided to take the kids to another pumpkin patch and let them each pick out one of their very own. Jessi picked out a big one, and Boone picked out a little one. He absolutely loved it—he even slept with it! It was always by his side the days before his accident. He even wanted to take a bath with it, but that's when I put my foot down and said, "Enough is enough."

My parents came down to the house to help Boone and Jessica carve their pumpkins. At first Boone tried to hide his, but he finally gave in and let his grandpa carve a little smiley face into the pumpkin. Boone was amazed at how it looked. When we put a candle inside and lit it, the look on Boone's face was priceless. He just stared in amazement.

I was able to hold Boone again that day. This time he was awake, and we cuddled and hugged and talked and told secrets to each other. It felt so good. He was fully aware of everyone and everything. We continued to quiz him on anything we knew that was important to him. Every answer was precise and perfect.

During these first six days at the hospital, we got to know a few of the other people who had children in the ICU ward. The couple whose little girl had her brain tumor removed on the day of Boone's accident were Christians, just like us. It was such a joy to see the faith and hope they had in their daughter's recovery. We kept each other updated on our children's conditions, and we gave support to one another. Jessica even became friends with the little girl, Colleen.

Boone's accident emboldened us to speak freely about the miracles of our Lord Jesus. That was something Randy and I were never able to do before. I suppose we were afraid of being rejected or laughed at. But now, God gave us ample reason to speak out. We jumped at any chance to share with others our experience with Boone and with God's true love.

A nun from the hospital came to visit us later in the day. As we shared our experience with her, she just sat at the edge of her chair and listened. Later on she suggested to me that I should consider writing about Boone's accident. I chuckled to myself. Ironically, I was in the middle of a writing course when the accident happened. She advised me to keep a journal about everything that was going on in Boone's life, and I did.

When it was time to say good night to Boone, I said, "I love you, Boone."

He looked up at me with his big blue eyes and said, "You love me?"

"Oh yes I do," I said.

"Oh!" he replied.

Boone was just starting to form sentences in his speech. He was a little late in speaking, partly because his sister would always talk for him.

After our nightly visitors left, Randy and I got out our pillows and blankets and stretched out on our couches in the lobby. The next day was going to be a very big day. It was Boone's third birthday.

Boone's Third Birthday

CHAPTER 4

The sun came up on November 4, and I rushed through my shower and my breakfast in anticipation of seeing my birthday boy. Boone was awake when I got to his room. I greeted him with a big, "Happy Birthday, Boone."

"Today is your birthday," I said. "You're three years old."

"My birthday?" he asked.

Boone often responded to a statement with a question, as if he were amazed by the information he just received.

The nurses were well aware that today was Boone's birthday, and they wanted him to look his best. They gave him a sponge bath and washed his hair.

My mom came to visit early that morning. Our plan was to have her take me home so that I could pick up a few presents we had for Boone and a birthday cake we had on order. We took off from the hospital and headed toward home.

While driving, mom and I talked about how well Boone was progressing. My mom was the best supporter that I had. I knew I could always count on her for anything. She was always willing to take the initiative to get things done the right way. Her encouragement and support is what helped me to get through the rough times.

As we approached my house, I felt a chill. I could still visualize Boone's accident. Even with his good progress, the shock of that moment still affected me.

I stayed at home just long enough to take a hot bath and pack a bag of clean clothes for Randy and me to wear at the hospital. Mom and I drove into town to pick up Boone's cake, then picked Jessica up from school on our way back to the hospital.

During our away time, Boone was moved to a different area in the ICU. Another baby wasn't doing very well. Boone was stable, and they needed the private room for the other child.

Jessica and I approached Boone with a handful of presents. He was very excited to see them. It was the best I had seen him yet. He still wasn't strong enough to sit up, so we had to help him open his presents.

All around him were signs of celebration. The nurses left a card for him on his table. A hospital employee brought in a banner that said "Happy Birthday." Lots of balloons were delivered that day, along with a few bouquets of flowers. Everyone made his day special. All the excitement wore Boone down. We had to shorten our usual visiting time to let him sleep.

Lots of family and friends came to wish Boone a happy birthday that evening. Only a few family members were allowed to see him personally. Boone received many presents, mostly stuffed animals. Soon, the inside of his crib was lined with a menagerie. I brought in his favorite rubber snake from home and hung it from his IV holder. It was hilarious to see how the nurses reacted when they discovered it. Their responses always made Boone giggle.

Boone was still in critical condition, but improving. He wasn't able to sit up yet because he was weak and his equilibrium was off. He hadn't been given anything solid to eat for over a week, but the nurses encouraged us to feed him a little of the ice cream we brought in for his birthday. He loved it, but didn't eat much of it. We gave each nurse a piece of cake and then took the rest out to the lobby for our visitors. The cake, by the way, was an Ewok cake. Boone loved the Ewoks.

The nurses encouraged us to celebrate Boone's birthday as if he was at home. Unfortunately, the celebration ended a bit short. As we were distributing the cake in the lobby, a nurse called Randy and I back into the ICU. She told us that they needed to send Boone downstairs for another CAT scan and another spinal tap test. Boone was running a low fever. They suspected an infection somewhere. The threat of meningitis returned, and fear came over us. Boone's birthday party quickly turned into a prayer session.

The nurses wheeled Boone to the patient elevator, right past all of our visitors. It was the first time anyone outside of the family was able to see him. He was wide awake, able to recognize all the familiar faces in the lobby. Seeing his two small cousins, Theron and Elisha, made his day. He was very close to his cousins, and they hadn't been able to visit him yet.

He enjoyed all the "hellos" and "how are you doings" he received while waiting for the elevator. Randy and I were a little nervous that someone with a cold or a virus would get too close to him and infect him. Thankfully, no one passed anything along to him.

Once the elevator doors closed and Boone was out of sight, everyone comforted us by telling us how well he looked. Shortly thereafter, people started to leave for home. Despite the scare at the end, Boone's birthday was a big success, though not the party we envisioned for his third birthday. There were no pony rides, no climbing on hay bales and running around in the barns, but there was a beautiful sense of knowing he was alive and coming along well.

By the time Boone was brought back upstairs, our visitors had all left. He opened a couple more presents before it was time to sleep. It was a big day for him, trying to answer everyone's questions at the elevator and knowing it was his birthday.

Back in the lobby, Randy and I talked about how well the day went. The CAT scan results would be available in the morning. We would have to wait another long seventy-two hours for the results of the spinal tap. Without hesitation, we turned to God. Before we said good night to each other, we prayed that Boone's test results would bring good news.

***

The lights inside the lobby turned on at their usual time, 6:30 AM. We woke up and visited Boone right away. We were anxious to see the "head doctor" to find out what the CAT scan showed. The nurse told us he wouldn't be there until eight o'clock, so we went ahead and took our showers and ate breakfast. When we returned to the ICU, the doctor was waiting for us. He told us the bruised area in Boone's cerebellum shrank. Things were healing well. Boone showed no more signs of leaking spinal fluid. The doctor was quite pleased with these results. Another test revealed that Boone's low fever was caused from a bladder infection, a result of the catheter he had been hooked up to. We were relieved to know that the infection was caused by something other than meningitis.

My parents were with us in the hospital that morning, so we decided to get some coffee while Boone rested. Before taking off, we stopped at the chapel and prayed once again. In my mind, I kept clinging to 1 Corinthians 10:13. Boone was still not completely out of the woods, but I knew God wouldn't let him die. God wouldn't let me live with the guilt. I would never, never be able to forgive myself for the accident. My emotions once again stirred inside of me.

Each one of us took turns at prayer. I prayed to Jesus that He would put His healing hand on Boone's little body, just to touch it with His healing power and make Boone better. During my time of prayer, I felt a sense of conviction. I knew God had given Boone to Randy and me to raise him in the knowledge and love of Christ as best we could. We raised Boone with lots and lots of love, but we fell short in raising him in a relationship with God. We went to church and prayed at meal times, but we never really took the time to teach our children about spiritual things. I knew this needed to change.

As we sat there in the quiet, peaceful chapel, tears began to drip off my cheeks. I prayed to God the hardest prayer I had ever prayed. *"Dear God. I pray to you Father and ask for Your healing hand to be upon Boone. Just to touch him with Your healing power is all I am asking. I don't know why this accident has happened, but I pray that You will use it for Your glory. Help Randy and me to share Your love to others and be a witness for You. I know you gave us Boone as our child and I know that he is your child as well. I give him back to you if that is Your will. I won't give him back peacefully, but I want what you want! If it means taking him from us then he is yours to take. But you also know that I want to keep him. Please help all of us through this horrible time. In Jesus' Precious name I pray. Amen!"*

What could I do? Physically there was nothing I could do. He was in the doctor's care. Spiritually, I could pray. But in the end, God was his Spiritual Doctor. What better care could I have possibly put him in? Boone had the best of both doctors on each side. The outcome of the situation was totally out of my hands.

I knew God wanted to see how much I would trust Him. I was willing to accept God's will for Boone, even if it meant He took my boy to heaven. Through it all, 1 Corinthians 10:13 was in my mind. I felt that if Boone was meant to die,

God would have taken him at the beginning of the ordeal. He wouldn't have allowed him to progress as well if He wasn't going to spare my son. God knew that we loved Boone as much as anything can be loved. We knew that God loved Boone even more than we did. He was asking us to trust Him fully with the life of our son, to let Him do a miracle. Randy and I both had to come to a place of surrender in prayer. As we placed our full faith and trust in Christ, a heaviness was lifted from us. We were assured that God knew we wanted our son back, whole and fit and new.

***

On that particular day, one of the babies in the pediatric ICU wasn't responding to medical attention. The child was kept alive by machines. I didn't really know anything about the baby's condition, except that it was dying. The parents had to make a decision about whether to keep the baby on life support or to let the baby pass.

Patti was at the hospital during this time. She took Jessica and her own children down the hall to a large play area. The family of the dying baby was in the playroom. Patti was overcome with a sense of sorrow as she kept noticing them watch our children play. She walked over to the couple and asked them if there was anything she could do for them. She specifically offered to pray with them. To Patti's surprise, they said no.

Patti was quite perplexed by their response, and so was I. We couldn't understand how someone could deny God's comfort, especially when their baby was dying. Prayer was the one thing that was pulling me through. I would not have endured my trial without the continual sense of God's presence and divine control. I knew He wasn't going to let us down, not with so many people that were praying for Boone. I knew what the Bible said:

Again, I tell you that if two of you on earth agree about anything you ask for, it will be done for you by my Father in heaven. For where two or three come together in my name, there am I with them. (Matthew 18:19 & 20)

About three years earlier, Randy and I took part in an eighteen-month Bible study. Part of our study was scripture memorization. I was always one of the best at memorizing verses. During Boone's accident, many of the verses I memorized kept coming to mind. Verses like Mark 11:24 were a constant reassurance: *"Therefore I tell you, whatever you ask for in prayer, believe that you have received it, and it will be yours."*

I knew what the Bible said about prayer. I didn't want anyone to stop praying for Boone. The more the merrier. I just couldn't understand how anyone could refuse an offer for prayer.

***

I was getting tired of staying at the hospital, so I decided to go home with my folks one night for a good night's sleep. Randy once again stayed behind.

It was early evening when we got to my parent's. A steaming hot bath was a source of relaxation for me that night. As I relaxed in the tub, I wondered how all Boone's injuries would turn out. After my bath, I went straight to bed at eight o'clock. I was out for the remainder of the night.

The next morning, I went down to my house and got some more clothes for Randy and me. My mom had some errands to run in town before we went back to the hospital, so I went with her. While we were in town, I remembered that about two weeks before Boone's accident, I had his pictures taken at a local drug store. We went to the store to pick up the pictures. I was so excited to see them. As the lady laid out the different shots of Boone, Mom and I just started to cry. All of Boone's pictures were perfect. It wasn't too often that Boone would smile for the camera, but in each picture, his smile was priceless. My mom explained to the lady what had happened to Boone. She became teary-eyed with us. The people standing in line behind surely wondered why three grown women were crying, but we didn't care what they thought. We were having a special moment.

We left the store with Boone's pictures and drove back to the hospital. Upon arrival, it appeared things were getting a little hectic. Boone's liquids (potassium and sodium) were out of whack. I wasn't aware of any prior issues with his liquid intake, but Randy said that the "liquid doctor" was concerned about his condition. I thought, *Oh, dear God, what now? I thought everything was supposed to be fine and improving.* A whole new set of new problems had developed.

Randy and I comforted each other. As we talked, we realized that the night before, when Randy was at the hospital and I was at my parent's house, we had each prayed the same exact prayer. We asked for whatever God's will was concerning Boone. I don't think all parents can say that they would pray the same for a child. When your child is healthy and normal, it's easy to say that you want what's best for him or her. But when your child is in critical condition in an ICU ward and the outcome is uncertain, saying to God, *"Whatever you want concerning my child,"* is a different story. It could mean losing your baby.

When we learned of Boone's new setback, we wondered to ourselves if maybe the Lord was going to take our son. In a way, I regretted the prayer—I didn't want to give Boone up. But God knew that before I even prayed. He knew we loved Boone dearly. The Lord was using this accident to prove that He is a loving and kind God to those who love Him. We held on to the word of Apostle Paul in:

Romans 8:28: "And we know that in all things God works for the good of those who love him, who have been called according to his purpose."

The "liquid doctor" was very busy that day with Boone. His potassium and sodium levels were causing all sorts of problems. The treatment for one was the opposite for the other. By the afternoon, Boone's condition wasn't getting any better. The doctor informed us that he was sending some specialists over to look at Boone and to give their diagnosis of what was going on. The problem he had was a condition called "diabetes insipidus." In order to comply with this condition, Boone had to take a specific medicine in order for his potassium and sodium levels to work in his body. Without this medicine, Boone continued to urinate with very little concentration in it.

I couldn't comprehend all that was being explained to us. My main concern was whether my son was going to live or not. I remember one doctor saying that his growth and development may not proceed as it should as he grows older.

We were all standing around Boone's crib as these specialists explained to us Boone's condition. The "liquid doctor" interrupted the conversation and asked us to step outside while he talked with the other doctors. Randy and I were puzzled. We waited in the lobby with the rest of my family. The "liquid doctor" came out and asked to speak to Randy and me alone. He explained to us that there had been an error in the pharmacy. The wrong IV solution was being administered to Boone. He went on to say that he had racked his brain all day wondering why the fluid levels suddenly went off the charts. His last resort was to have the IV solution analyzed.

We looked at each other thinking, *how could that have happened?* When the doctor left, we told the family the news. As our family stood around and talked about this situation, we realized that humans make mistakes. That includes doctors, nurses, pharmacists, and lab technicians. Maybe we would have had different feelings if harm had come to our son through their mistake, but we were just thankful that the problem was found and being corrected.

Boone's life was all we cared about. God was giving it back to us.

A Big Surprise

CHAPTER 5

W hen we awoke the next morning, the nurses told us that Boone had a very peaceful night's sleep. I was glad to hear this, considering all that his little body went through the day before. When we were allowed back to the ICU that morning, we were surprised to see Boone sitting in a high chair next to the nurse's station with jam all over his face! I couldn't help but laugh at the sight. It was such a joy to see him out of his bed. He had been sitting up for only a few minutes at a time during the previous days, and that was with constant supervision. During those times, he would get dizzy and act as if he were hurting. For me to see him sitting in a high chair was a *big* surprise. It was also a great joy to see how well he had eaten. For breakfast that morning he had two eggs, three pieces of toast, and a full box of milk.

He looked at me when I entered the room and said, "Hi, Mama!"

"Hi Boone," I replied, "What a big boy you are!"

"Yeah," he said.

I could tell that Boone was tired after eating his breakfast. He had never sat up that long before. His equilibrium was unstable still, and he would get dizzy easily. The nurse took him out of his high chair and laid him back in his bed.

While he lay there, the nurse washed the jam from his face. He was ready to drift off for a morning nap.

His black eye was well healed by now, and the swelling was way down. The stitches above his eye and by his belly button (where they had done a probe to look for internal injuries) had all been removed.

While his eye was swollen, he was able to wink easily. We laughed at him the first time he did it. He thought it was funny. From that point on, Boone winked at all the nurses. They thought it was cute, of course, and they took a real liking to him.

Boone continued to get better every day. Other children were coming and going through the ICU regularly. I can tell you from experience that after you see so many children and tiny babies fighting such intense illnesses, you come to admire the strength children possess.

The day soon arrived when Boone was released from the ICU. All of Boone's tests had come back negative, and there had been no more spinal fluid leaking from his nose or from anywhere else. Boone was well enough to be moved upstairs to the pediatric ward on the fifth floor. We were excited about the move, but at the same time we were afraid he wouldn't get the same quality of care as he had in the ICU, where he had one nurse dedicated to his care during each shift.

We gathered all of his balloons, stuffed animals, and flowers to take to his new room. There were so many that we had to make multiple trips just to get them all moved. Then we finally settled Boone into his new room. At this point, Boone was upgraded from critical condition to serious condition.

It was much more relaxing for us in the pediatric ward. Boone had his own room with a TV and sink and chairs. We were now able to sleep in the same room with him. (We actually got cots to sleep on too!) The pediatric ward had a playroom, which was great for Jessica. She could go in the playroom and help the other children paint or play, what-ever their needs were. We were starting to feel like a family again.

Boone's eating habits continued to improve, and we were able to eat with him in his room. He began to sit up pretty well by himself, but he was still wobbly. We wouldn't let him sit up unless the crib sides were up and the pillows were bordered around his crib.

Visitors from outside of the family were now welcome in the room with Boone. This was a relief to me. I no longer felt the need to entertain visitors. I could now tend to Boone's needs at the same time I chatted with our guests.

One special visitor that came to see Boone was Mike, the pilot who flew the helicopter that brought our son to the hospital. He was stationed just around the corner from the pediatric ward, so one day he came in for a visit. Mike became a dear friend to us. We even called him "Uncle Mike." He informed us that only twelve minutes had passed from the time he received the call for Life Flight to the time he landed the helicopter in our field. This was an amazing fact to learn. To drive the distance he flew would have taken well over an hour. Uncle Mike gave Boone some pictures of the Life Flight helicopter, a T-shirt, a Life Flight pin, and some stickers. He became a frequent and much welcomed visitor.

Boone lost weight after the accident, so we worked on getting him to eat heartily to gain some weight. Breakfast was always his best meal. It wasn't uncommon for him to drink two small cartons of milk and to eat three pieces of toast, a bowl of cheerios, and two scrambled eggs. I couldn't believe he could consume so much food at once, but he did. He ate less at lunch and dinner (probably because he was still full from breakfast).

Boone progressed steadily. He was soon upgraded from serious condition to stable condition. The worst was over.

The Good Lord had given us back our son. I was especially relieved to know that Boone's brain was functioning properly. This was evidenced by the fact that Boone was talking more now than he had ever talked before. His newfound talkativeness was largely due to the fact that the nurses and doctors required him to answer their many questions. Sometime soon, Boone would be back to throwing cats in the swimming pool, playing with horse poop, squeezing slugs, and doing the other typical little boy things he was doing a month before.

The day came when it was time to remove the "grand central station" from Boone's neck. This was a large port installed in his neck for the doctors and nurses to draw blood and administer his meds without poking him all the time with needles. It was a relief to have absolutely no tubes connected to our son anymore. He was healing well. By this point, the only medicine he needed was for the diabetes insipidus he developed as a result of the trauma to his brain.

It was now time for a new group of doctors to examine our son. We scheduled an "eye doctor" and an "ear doctor" to come in.

I remember trying to whisper to Boone to see if he could hear me. At times he could, but there were times when he acted confused. I suspected there might be some sort of hearing problem, but I wasn't sure how severe.

In his left eye, partial paralysis was noticeable. If he tried to turn his eyes to the left, his right eye would move just fine. His left eye just looked straight ahead. Also, when he cried, no tears came out of his left eye.

He was still having a problem with his fluids, a result of the diabetes insipidus. Here's how the condition is best described:

Diabetes insipidus is sometimes called "water diabetes" because a person is constantly thirsty and has a tendency to put out urine that appears to be clear-colored. It involves the posterior pituitary gland (which Boone injured in his accident). It develops when a person is unable to produce a necessary secretion in the pituitary glad. This affects the kidneys, making it difficult for someone to properly balance the amount of fluid that must be reabsorbed into the body's circulatory system and the amount that is passed out of the body as urine. As this disease progresses it causes constipation, dry skin, loss of weight and appetite. A person with diabetes insipidus is constantly thirsty and frequently needs to urinate. The disease can cause other conditions as well.

In order to control Boone's condition, he was administered a very small drop of clear liquid called DDAVP by blowing it from a tube into his nose. Many patients respond well to this medicine.

We were told that when Boone was released from the hospital, Randy and I would have to monitor his fluids and give him the medicine when needed. I wasn't sure I would be able to administer the meds; he always had nurses and doctors to do these things. But I figured I wouldn't worry about it until the time came.

The next couple of days were spent showering Boone with lots of love and attention. When Jessica came to the hospital, we got a little red wagon that was specifically made for the patients who couldn't walk. It was such a treat for Boone to be able to ride in it. Jessica loved pulling Boone around the ward and showing him off.

On the day that the "eye doctor" and the "ear doctor" were scheduled to check Boone, I decided to go home for a few hours to pay some bills and to prepare the house for Boone's homecoming. I hadn't driven a vehicle for over two weeks, and I knew I had to get over the fear I now had of being behind the wheel.

When I put the key in the ignition, I suddenly visualized Boone lying in a mud puddle. I prayed to God to help me overcome these images and for guidance to drive home safely. With His help, I found the strength to drive again.

When I got home, Randy called to say that the "eye doctor" wanted me to pick up an eye patch to cover Boone's right eye, his good eye. This would help strengthen his left eye, which was indeed partially paralyzed. Thankfully, he had perfect vision in both eyes, despite being unable to control the side movement of his left eye.

Randy also informed me that the "ear doctor" performed a simple test to determine if there was any hearing disability. She discovered that there was some hearing loss in Boone's left ear, but she wasn't sure how much or if there was loss in the right ear as well. She wanted us to set up an appointment to have a complete hearing test done at a nearby clinic before we took him home.

When Randy told me what the "ear doctor" said, I felt nauseous. Guilt once again came upon me. I thought to myself, *Look what you have done. You caused Boone to have hearing loss.* I wondered if there would ever be an end to his problems and to my guilty feelings.

As I headed back to the hospital, I stopped by an eye clinic and bought a black eye patch for Boone. I thought Boone would get a kick out of wearing this patch, but to my surprise, he didn't like it at all. We tried playing pirates. I wore it; Randy wore it; but Boone just didn't like it. We had to do some quick talking to get his attention focused on something else in order to get him to wear his patch. Eventually, he complied.

The last couple of days that Boone was in the hospital, Randy and I were taught how to monitor his diabetes insipidus. It was confusing at first, but the more we practiced, the more it became routine. Some doctors said he should eventually produce the hormone he needed to recover; others said he might never recover. Regardless, he had to be monitored closely. Any weight loss of one-half to one pound was reason to seek medical attention.

Boone was such a good boy in the hospital. In a way he was like a baby again. He couldn't walk and he wore a diaper, yet he was so much more talkative than he had ever been. His ability to concentrate had developed tremendously. He was using his energy in different ways than he had before. He was now able to sit for hours and put together puzzles designed for six to eight year olds.

After nineteen days at Boone's side, we heard the best words ever: "Well, it looks like you'll be able to go home today." We were so happy! Just a few weeks prior, we weren't sure whether Boone was going to live or die. Now, he was coming home.

Boone needed one more test before going home, the hearing test. We drove him ourselves to a different hospital building. When we got there, we wrapped him up in a blanket and carried him to the elevator. A lady in the elevator looked at Boone and said, "You look like a tough little guy," remarking about the scar over his eye and the dark circles under both eyes. Randy and I looked at each other with smiles on our faces. All I said to her was, "You have no idea."

The "ear doctor" had me go into a soundproof room with Boone. There was a little table inside with headphones for Boone to wear. The doctor brought out little toys, such as a cowboy, an Indian, a cat, and a dog. Boone was to point to the toy that she would call out over the headphones. The test results concluded that Boone had good hearing in his right ear but none at all in the left ear. Once again, guilt came over me.

The doctor said that Boone's type of injury affected the nerves on the inside of his eardrum. She informed us that surgery was not an option. On the upswing, she said he would never have to go to war because of his hearing impairment. With that little phrase about war, I felt a sense of relief. It was a blessing in disguise. I took the news as a sign of God protecting my son from future danger. I knew in my heart that the hearing loss was something we could deal with.

We left the doctor's office and headed back to the hospital. In a few hours, we'd be taking Boone home with us.

Home Sweet Home

CHAPTER 6

Boone's release day was on a Friday. I was instructed to bring him back for a checkup on Monday. Randy made several trips to the truck before we left the hospital, hauling all of Boone's toys, flowers, and balloons. We bundled Boone up, said "good-bye" and "thank you" to the staff, and headed out the door. Back home, my mom and Jessi were waiting for us with balloons and a huge banner taped to the wall: WELCOME HOME BOONE! Boone was finally out of the hospital—Thank you, God!

Boone couldn't walk yet, so my mom brought over a huge beanbag chair for him to recline on. We put a sheepskin blanket that the hospital had given to him on the beanbag chair and positioned him in front of the TV. It was the perfect support for his little body.

It was a special night for our family. We were all able to sleep in the house at the same time, something we hadn't done in almost three weeks. It was a restless night for Randy and me as we got up to check on Boone at least once every half hour.

When morning came, we needed to weigh Boone and monitor his fluid input/output levels. As the day went on, we continued checking him. When the time came to give him medicine, we were nervous that we were going to mess up, but everything worked out fine. We could tell that the medicine was working; therefore, we knew we had followed the doctor's instructions properly. We had to write down every time he went potty, how much he urinated, and how much fluid he drank.

In the evenings, Randy and I worked with Boone to help him walk again. He wanted to walk, but he just couldn't at first, so he decided to crawl. Nothing was going to slow him down. When he wanted something, he wanted it *now*. He was acting like the little boy that he was before.

By Sunday night, just two days after being discharged from the hospital, he was walking by himself. We knew the doctor would be impressed come Monday.

Our first weekend back home passed, and it was time to report back for his follow-up appointment. The doctor said that everything appeared to be great. He told us that we were keeping very good records on Boone's progress.

Three weeks after he was released from the hospital, Boone was scheduled for physical therapy as an outpatient at a hospital near our home. The therapist put him through many physical tests. At the end of the session, she told us that if she hadn't known what type of accident he had been in, she would never have known anything was wrong with him, except for a tight right hamstring. No physical therapy was needed for him at all.

Praise God, I thought. To think, only three weeks prior, our son couldn't even walk. Now a physical therapist couldn't find anything wrong with him. This was truly a miracle.

Boone's bad eye started to move a little more to the left, and at times he could move it all the way over. The eye doctor said that Boone would get back all of his movement, but she was more concerned with his "dry eye" situation. We were advised to put fake teardrops in his eyes three times a day and to lubricate them at night with some special medicine. She said she didn't think he had much feeling in his left eye. We were to watch it carefully so that nothing could get in it and irritate it. Over time, Boone's eye did recover its full movement from left to right. To this day, he still has problems with dry eye, and he does not produce tears in that one eye.

We needed to take Boone to a local hospital for a blood test that would check on his electrolytes. The doctors needed to know his levels of sodium, potassium, and bicarbonates. If they were too low or too high, the doctor would possibly need to change his medications.

Our son was so sick and tired of being stabbed with needles. It didn't help that it was difficult to find a vein in his arm that was large enough to draw blood from. On the day of the blood test, he was fine until he saw the needle. He screamed and cried. It took three nurses and one doctor to hold him down. It took them twenty minutes to get two little vials of blood. I had to leave the room because I was getting faint listening to him plead for my help. I just couldn't take any more. I broke down and cried. The nurses were very sympathetic with him, and they showered him with lots and lots of stickers, which he was very proud of.

The test results of his electrolytes came back, and they were off a little bit, so we continued to monitor his blood. During the first six weeks that Boone was home from the hospital, he had twelve doctor appointments. It was a lot, but every time we went, I was assured he was getting better. The main problem was still his diabetes insipidus, so we continued to monitor his fluids and medication accordingly.

The Christmas season was upon us. Our church has a special tradition where certain children are asked to light the Christmas candles for the evening services throughout December. Boone and Jessica were asked to light the candles one Sunday. It was such a joy to see Boone walk down the aisle all by himself and try to light the candles. He had a little problem with one candle. When he started to get a little frustrated, I walked up and helped him light it. He and Jessica then walked back down the aisle. I walked to the back of the church to greet the kids, but Boone didn't see me. He ran back down the church aisle hollering, "Mama, Mama, where are you?" It was so cute to watch him full of spirit. The entire church enjoyed the moment as well.

One evening my sister and brother-in-law were going to take Randy and me out for dinner to break up our schedule. She had a babysitter all lined up for us. When Patti came to pick us up, Glenn wasn't with her. She said that he got home late from work and needed to take a shower. We would swing by her house to pick him up on the way to the restaurant.

Back to Patti's house we traveled. She said that we might as well come in for a minute; Glenn wouldn't be ready yet. As we walked through the door, people all at once yelled, "Surprise!" They had arranged a surprise thirtieth birthday party. My birthday, which was on Christmas Day, was three days away.

It was a great party and a much needed escape for me. My family and friends kept teasing me that I was going to go into labor while the party was going on, but I wasn't due for ten more days. I was planning on a New Year's baby.

When Randy and I got home, I crawled into bed and at 11:08 PM (I remember looking at the clock). I no sooner lay down to go to sleep when I felt my contractions starting. I made a quick call to my folks and readied to leave for the hospital. We had discussed earlier with my folks that we wanted my mom to come to the hospital and bring Jessica with her so that she could take part in the delivery. Mom picked up Jessica while my dad took Boone back to their home to finish sleeping.

I checked in to the hospital, and while I was getting undressed in my room, my mom and Jessica arrived. With only one other lady and baby in the whole maternity ward, we got lots of attention. My mom and Jessica were in my room during labor, which helped me to concentrate on something else instead of my pain.

It took only two hours after the first contraction until I was ready to push. Randy, Mom, and Jessica were all in their green uniforms, scrubbed and standing by my side in the delivery room.

I was kind of hoping for a girl. I felt that no other boy would compare to my little Boone, especially after all that we had gone through together. But at 1:48 AM, I delivered a very healthy, eight-pound, two-and-a-half ounce baby boy. Exactly two hours and forty minutes after my first contraction began. *Thank you, Jesus!*

My mom was the first to hold Brett R. Noble. (In case you're wondering, Brett's middle name is just an initial: *R.* This is because relatives on both sides of our family have names that start with the *R*: Randy, Russell (my dad), Roy (Randy's dad), and Ren (my grandfather). We decided to honor them all.

Mom beamed with joy and told me over and over again how beautiful and round baby Brett was. Jessica could only giggle. Once I held my new baby boy and saw how chubby and beautiful he was, I was overwhelmed. I knew the Lord had His reasons for giving us another boy.

On the evening of the same day, Boone came in to see me with Jessica and Randy. I was so afraid Randy wouldn't monitor Boone's fluids and that my boy would end up back in the hospital, but I didn't need to worry. Randy did just fine. Boone was glad to see me and happy to have a little brother.

On Christmas Day, my birthday, the doctor released us to go home. I noticed as the kids came in my room that Randy had taken them shopping. Jessica came proudly strutting into the room wearing a beautiful soft blue dress. Next came Boone, racing in through the doors, looking like such a big boy, all dressed up in a three-piece suit with a tie. He looked so grown-up that I started to cry.

After I ate breakfast and packed my bag, we got Brett all snuggled up in some pajamas and a blanket. The hospital had made giant Christmas socks for the babies to go home in. They were really cute.

When we left the hospital, we went to Randy's sister's house for dinner and to open presents. We then proceeded to our house for our own Christmas. It was such a relief to be home, all snuggled on the couch with the new baby, my other two children, and Randy. It was a wonderful Christmas, considering all that had happened in the last six weeks. I thanked God for His blessings.

***

Boone had nothing to do with me or the baby for the first couple of days. He was pretty jealous, and it made me feel absolutely horrible that he didn't even want to sit by me. By the third day, he realized that the baby wasn't going back to the hospital and that he was there to stay. That is when he finally decided to talk to me (but not to the baby).

Boone continued to get stronger. He was definitely back to his old habits, demanding things here and now with zero patience.

One day, I had a follow-up appointment with the doctor who delivered Brett. As I waited for him to come in the room, I sat on the table thinking about Boone's accident and all the things that happened within the last couple months. Just as my emotions were welling up, the doctor came in. I managed to hold my feelings back while he did his checkup. He said I looked great, and I didn't need to come back. Nonchalantly, he asked me how Boone was doing. All of a sudden, I burst into tears for no reason at all. I caught the doctor off guard with my emotional outburst.

The doctor suggested it might be good to talk to a counselor he knew. It would be good for me to let some of my feelings out. I agreed, and he gave me her business card.

I didn't want anyone to know how much grief I had inside me. I knew I needed to let out my frustrations and anxieties. While I was pregnant, I hadn't allowed myself to breakdown. Now that my emotions were bursting out, I realized it was time to deal with them.

When I met my counselor, she asked me many questions about Boone and the accident. I found myself opening up to her in a way I thought was impossible. We talked about a number of problems I faced daily. The first was the picture I still had in my mind of Boone in my rear view mirror, laying in that mud puddle. Another was the phantom bumps I felt whenever I was driving, as though I was running over someone again and again. The counselor helped me to get over my feelings of guilt, and she helped me realize that children are very active and very curious. In my case, it happened to be that Boone was just a curious little boy who wanted out of a truck to go play in a mud puddle. She always ended my sessions by giving me a poem that lifted me up.

I had a very hard time forgiving myself and releasing my guilt. This lady was patient and understanding. She told me that I needed to look at myself as if I were another person to see if I would like me. That's when things began to click for me. Still, forgiving myself was one of the hardest things I had to do.

While I was working with the counselor, Boone was developing behavioral patterns that needed to change. Boone was getting used to being waited on hand and foot. I didn't mind waiting on him until he started throwing fits when he didn't get his way. All the doctors told us it was time to treat him like a normal boy again and not to baby him so much. (Easier said than done!) Randy and I went together as a couple to talk with the counselor a few times. She helped us form a strategy on how best to discipline Boone.

I continued to write about Boone's accident, which was good therapy for me. One day the counselor informed me that I didn't need to come back to her any longer. An overwhelming sense of achievement overcame me as I heard those words. I felt as though I conquered a self inflicted sense of grief and came through this tragedy with a strong belief that miracles happen.

Boone was starting to show signs that his fluids were returning to normal. He needed his medicine less frequently than before. We prayed so much for the Lord to restore his hormones.

On March 23, 1986, we went to a church that had prayed for Boone many times. Randy and I were trying to make follow-up visits to the churches that had prayed for our little boy. We wanted to show them what the power of prayer accomplished for us. People were thrilled to see how well he had recovered.

The church we visited on that particular day asked if we would mind if they prayed over Boone's body for healing. As we took Boone to the front of the church, a group of people came forward, laid their hands on him, and prayed in the name of Jesus Christ and His healing power to mend Boone's hormones. I believed God would answer our prayers at that very moment. Miraculously, starting that Sunday, Boone never again needed to take medication for his diabetes insipidus. What a glorious day this was for us. We continued to keep records on Boone's fluids for another week, but he simply did not need any medication. What a miracle!

God's Grace, Our Gratitude

CHAPTER 7

The month of June arrived and Boone had a couple of follow-up doctor's appointments back at the hospital. The "head doctor" said Boone looked fine and there was no need for him to come back unless he injured his head again. He made it clear, however, that Boone should never be permitted to play football, water polo, boxing, or any sport that involved hard contact with the head. He also said that Boone should not be permitted to ride a bike until he was at a responsible age. Riding a bicycle takes tremendous balance. The doctor thought with the imbalance that comes with hearing loss in one ear, Boone could easily injure himself. With those instructions, we no longer needed to see the "head doctor" again.

The last follow-up was with the "ear doctor." She said that no change in his hearing had been detected. We didn't need to come back to her either until Boone started school. At that time, we would need a letter from her stating that Boone needed to sit on the left side of the room towards the front of the class so that he could hear the teacher with his good ear.

Jessica's last day of kindergarten was June 6. We anticipated a great summer full of swimming and relaxation. My parents have an outdoor swimming pool that overlooks part of a huge valley. It was great to sit in the warmth of the sun and do nothing but float atop the pool and watch the kids play in the water.

Randy and I felt so grateful for all the hospital had done for us. We decided to have a party for all the people involved in Boone's rehabilitation. The "liquid doctor" came with his family, as did one of the pastors from our church, our entire family, and the man from 9-1-1. Uncle Mike drove out to our house early that day. He couldn't make the party because of work. We were at church when he showed up, so we missed him. He left a three-wheeled bike for Boone with a note that said he would fly over the house in the helicopter later in the day.

One person I was excited to meet was Loren, the 9-1-1 dispatcher. We talked about the day of Boone's accident. It was interesting to find out what my conversation was with him, as I wasn't aware at all of what I had said to him on the phone. It was amazing that God, from the very beginning, had control of the whole situation.

A little later we heard a helicopter approaching from over the hill. As we all lined up by the edge of the pool, we could see Uncle Mike coming. He flew low over the pool, and then he made a complete circle over us. We could see him inside the cockpit as he waved to us all. Boone was elated to see the helicopter; he was jumping around like he had ants in his pants. It was quite a day.

The sunny warm days of summer were coming to an end. Soon, school would start again. By now, Boone was brave enough to go down the waterslide by himself and jump off of the diving board, but he always had an inner tube vest on, since he didn't know how to swim. Jessi was a little fish. She learned on her own how to swim that summer, and at the age of six she learned how to dive off of the diving board. Then there was our seven-month-old son, Brett. He, too, loved the water.

September rolled around and Jessi was off to school, entering the first grade. I enrolled Boone in a preschool where he would attend two times a week for two-and-a-half hours. We knew it would be good for him to be around other kids and to take instructions from someone other than Mom and Dad. One activity he really enjoyed at preschool was making pictures for Mommy. Naturally, I loved them all! Each day when I picked him up from school, he looked up at me and said in the sweetest, most innocent voice, "I love my school." It made me grin from ear to ear.

I owe so much to God for all He has done for Boone and for giving us another chance with him. God knows we are human; therefore, we will make mistakes now and then. Never, never should a person give up hope. Hope is all we can live with in times of despair. God does listen to us when we pray, so by all means, we should never cease. The more people I knew who prayed for Boone, the better I knew he was going to be.

October was upon us, and it was an emotional time for me. It was one year prior that our disaster struck. We had big plans for Boone's birthday that year. We were going to celebrate to the utmost. Boone was excited about Halloween approaching. He had missed out the year before. We had already carved two pumpkins by the second week in October. I wondered how many pumpkins we would go through before Halloween arrived.

After one complete year of recovery, we went back to the hospital during the last week of October. We wanted to give pumpkin balloons to all the children in the pediatric ward, just as someone did for Boone when he was there. We greeted the nurses and told them why we were there. They accepted our gesture of gratitude and told us to go ahead. Some of the nurses remembered Boone, and they were so surprised at how he had progressed—walking, talking, and giggling!

As we visited each child in the pediatric ward, we tied balloons to the end of each bed. At each bed we saw a bit of a smile come from the kids, even though each was dealing with his or her own pains and physical struggles. Seeing these smiles come through, I remembered the day Boone saw his little orange pumpkin balloon tied to the end of his bed and the smile that came through all his pain. God loves His little children, and He used us that day to put smiles on their faces.

Psalms 116

*I love the Lord, for he heard my voice; he heard my
cry for mercy.*

*Because he turned his ear to me, I will call on him as
long as I live.*

*The cords of death entangled me, the anguish of the
grave came upon me; I was overcome by trouble
and sorrow.*

*Then I called on the name of the Lord: "O Lord, save
me!"*

*The Lord is gracious and righteous; our God is full
of compassion.*

*The Lord protects the simple-hearted, when I was in
great need, he saved me.*

*Be at rest once more, O my soul, for the Lord has
been good to you.*

*For you, O Lord, have delivered my soul from death,
my eyes from tears, my feet from stumbling, that
I may walk before the Lord in the land of the
living.*

I believed; therefore I said, "I am greatly afflicted."

And in my dismay I said, "All men are liars."

*How can I repay the Lord for all his goodness to
me?*

*I will lift up the cup of salvation and call on the name
of the Lord. I will fulfill my vows to the Lord in
the presence of all his people.*

*Precious in the sight of the Lord is the death of his
saints.*

*O Lord, truly I am your servant; I am your servant,
the son of your maidservant; you have freed me
from my chains.*

*I will sacrifice a thank offering to you and call on the
name of the Lord.*

I will fulfill my vows to the Lord in the presence of all his people, in the courts of the house of the Lord—in your midst, O Jerusalem. Praise the Lord.

ACKNOWLEDGEMENTS

To the many pastors that came and prayed with us and to our relatives and friends who gave support, I thank you from the bottom of my heart. We love you, and I don't think we could have made it without you.

Most of all, I thank God for His love and understanding of our needs. His presence was so close to us, and it still is. I don't think a day has gone by that I haven't been reminded of that horrible nightmare, but when I see Boone running around like any other child, I count my blessings.

Thank you, Lord, for hearing my many, many prayers and for answering them. My prayer now is that Boone will grow up to know you and to serve you and especially to love you with all his heart. Thank you again for giving him back to me. You are a God of love.

Boone's graduation from high school.

Jessica's Story
"HEAVEN BOUND"

Jessica, My Own Special Angel

CHAPTER 1

It was 1988, and Jessica was entering third grade. A week before school started, I drove Jessica to her school to see who was listed as her teacher for the year. She would either have the man teacher, Mr. Hageman, or the woman teacher, Miss Drennan. Jessica wanted Miss Drennan. She preferred female teachers to male teachers. We got in the van and drove down the road to Mulino Grade School, Jessica's only school since kindergarten.

When we arrived at the school, we walked first to the office area, where the class rosters were posted. We searched for her name to see which teacher she would get. We found her name on the roster for Mr. Hageman's class. I could tell by the look on Jessica's face that she was a little disappointed. But since she said nothing, I said nothing. We continued on with our visit, checking where her classroom was located and familiarizing ourselves with the wing in which it was located. After arriving back home, we began preparing for her first day of school—what to wear, how to fix her hair, and all the things little girls care about at the age of nine.

When the first day of school arrived, Jessica was excited to see all her friends. She was an excellent student, a role model for other kids. But she didn't start that way. Her birthday was on September 12, so she was young when she started kindergarten. She struggled her first year, so we decided to keep her in kindergarten one more year. This turned out to be a good decision. Jessica excelled in her schoolwork and came into her own as a result of going through kindergarten twice.

About a week after school started, Jessica came home with a puzzled look on her face.

"Mom, what's an atheist?" she asked me.

I was a little surprised to hear that word come out of the mouth of a nine year old.

"Where did you hear that word, Jessi?" I asked her.

"At school. Someone said Mr. Hageman is an atheist."

At this time, our family was very involved with church. I actually taught the Bible to Jessica's age group on Wednesday nights at the Molalla Conservative Baptist Church in Molalla, Oregon. I explained to her what an atheist was, and then I said to her, "Well, if you want to get Miss Drennan for your teacher, I will try to get you changed. Or, you can stay with Mr. Hageman. Maybe there is some unknown reason why you are supposed to have him as a teacher."

Jessica did not want to change teachers. She wanted to stay with Mr. Hageman. She was very open about her relationship with Jesus. If anyone could convert an atheist, it was her. She loved the Lord with all her heart. Her faith was a complete example of what the Bible says about having faith like a child:

> *At that time the disciples came to Jesus and asked, "Who is the greatest in the kingdom of heaven?" He called a little child and had him stand among them. And he said: "I tell you the truth, unless you change and become like little children, you will never enter the kingdom of heaven. Therefore, whoever humbles himself like this child is the greatest in the kingdom of*

heaven. And whoever welcomes a little child like this in my name welcomes me. But if anyone causes one of these little ones who believe in me to sin, it would be better for him to have a large millstone hung around his neck and to be drowned in the depths of the sea." (Matthew 18:1–6)

Then little children were brought to Jesus for him to place his hands on them and pray for them. But the disciples rebuked those who brought them. Jesus said, "Let the little children come to me, and do not hinder them, for the kingdom of heaven belongs to such as these." When he had placed his hands on them, he went on from there. (Matthew 19: 13–15)

During the summer leading into her third grade year, Jessica asked me if she could be baptized. I did not question if she understood the meaning of baptism at her young age. I knew she was well aware of what being baptized meant. So that summer she was baptized at the age of eight in Deardorff Lake, a beautiful and private lake in the hills of Molalla. Jessica attended church since she was a baby. She believed in God and accepted Him at a very young age. She shared her faith as only a child could to all her friends and family.

From a mother's eye, Jessica was a perfect little girl in all aspects. My relationship with her was awesome. She grew to be my best friend, not just my daughter. We shared many thoughts and feelings with each other. She loved to hear a bit of gossip now and then from her mama. When she did, she would always run to tell her grandma what the latest secret was. I had to be careful if I didn't want something blabbed.

During Jessica's first few weeks of third grade, her teacher created a program for his class that would honor students if they completed all their schoolwork, performed certain chores, and were well behaved. For each task they completed, he rewarded them by putting a sticker on their monthly chart. At the end of the month, the student who received the most stickers also received some sort of award to commemorate his or her success. Jessica won them all! She was the perfect role model for her peers.

One particular day she came home from school with her head hung low.

"What is the matter?" I asked her.

"I won the monthly sticker award again," she replied.

I was of course excited to hear that her success in her schoolwork and behavior was noticeable to her teacher once again. I couldn't understand why this was a cause for sadness.

"The other kids are mad at me because I always win," she told me.

"Honey, they're just jealous," I said. "You make them have to work harder in order to get the award. You're being a role model to them. You're inspiring them to put out more effort to get better grades."

This was hard for her to accept at first. She wanted their friendship, not for them to be mad at her. But once she thought about how she was setting the standard for her peers, I think she finally accepted the fact and was satisfied.

Jessica had two younger brothers, Boone and Brett. Brett, the youngest, was two years old when Jessica started third grade. He was the apple of Jessica's eye. She was Brett's second mama, and she was proud of it. She loved to show him off to her friends at school whenever I came to pick her up. And he loved all the attention. Boone, who turned six that year, was also a big part of Jessica's life. While Boone was recovering at home from a bad accident (the details of which are talked about in "Boone's Story") Jessica was his nurse, so to speak. In fact, after Boone's ordeal, she decided she wanted to become a nurse. She had a natural patience when it came to dealing with sick people in hospitals.

Earlier, when Boone was in the hospital for three weeks, Jessica befriended a girl her age who had been diagnosed with a brain tumor. The little girl kept falling down during gymnastics, so her parents took her to the doctor to get some testing done. It was then that they discovered a tumor in her brain. While this little girl was in the hospital, she would not eat and was unresponsive to others. One day, Jessica, while visiting her brother in the hospital, walked down the halls of the pediatric ward and looked into all the rooms of the other kids that were in recovery. When she saw this little girl, she went to her bedside and started talking to her. The little girl responded to Jessica. Her parents immediately picked up on the way Jessica impacted their daughter and asked us if she could come visit their daughter on a daily basis. Of course we allowed this. After a few visits, Jessica was able to get the little girl to start eating. It was such a blessing to see how she worked in this little girl's life. Our hearts were amazed by how her love was passed on to others. Many times I believed that Jessica was my angel, sent to earth for us all. I was amazed how a little nine year old had the heart (and at times the mind) of an adult. Her presence radiated love!

Jessica also communicated well with handicapped people, including people with mental disorders. Her Great Aunt Geraldine, my mother's only sibling, was mentally challenged. She lived in the Oregon State Hospital and other mental facilities most of her life. She suffered from anger outbursts and schizophrenia. It was too hard of a job for my grandmother to care for Auntie on a day-to-day basis. There were many times when Auntie's medications got out of whack and she would have sudden outbursts of anger. She would then be hospitalized for long periods of time. When she appeared to be stable for months, Auntie was allowed to come back home again. This went on for years, until Grandma couldn't do it any longer and had to place Geraldine permanently in a facility.

My mother and grandmother visited Aunt Geraldine on a weekly basis, and many times Jessica went with them. It was a special time for her to be with both her grandmas. Jessi would fixate on the different personalities of some of the patients, although she was at times bothered by their outbursts. I believe by her going often to visit, she developed a deep compassion for mentally challenged individuals. Jessi was aware at a very young age that people are different in many ways.

In January of 1989, Aunt Geraldine died. It was a sad time for all of us, but we knew Aunt Geraldine was in a better place. She would no longer suffer from the mental problems she endured her whole life. In preparing for the funeral, my sister Patti and I decided we would have the nieces and nephews get together and sing "Jesus Loves Me." We taped the children singing as opposed to having them sing at the funeral.

The day of the funeral approached, and Aunt Geraldine was lying in an open casket. I asked Jessica if she wanted to see Auntie. She was hesitant to do so at first, but later she decided to view the body. I remember it was the first time Jessica had seen death. While it was scary to her, she took comfort in knowing that Auntie wasn't hurting anymore. The time came for the kids' song to play. The recording sounded like little angels singing from heaven for their Auntie, something never to be forgotten.

Later that day, Jessica and I talked openly about Aunt Geraldine's life and how she was instantly in heaven with Jesus, with a new body, one that wasn't hurting anymore. Our conversation regarding death was soon to be put in front of me. I had no idea that Jessi would soon be reunited with her great aunt.

A Tragic Game

CHAPTER 2

Tuesday, February 14, 1989—Valentine's Day! Jessica and Boone were excited to go to school and celebrate the day. They looked forward to exchanging Valentine cards with their friends. Their excitement had been mounting for several days, and the big day was here at last.

It was a brisk winter day with no rain. I drove Jessica and Boone to school that morning to make sure their cards were delivered to each of their classmates' specially decorated Valentine folders. Brett, who was now three, was with us, enjoying all the fun and giggles we shared on that special day. Later that afternoon, I would hear all about the day's festivities when I took Jessica and Boone with me on a trip to Salem to deliver some paperwork to our accountant.

After my morning routine, I picked up Boone from kindergarten then went home to grab the paperwork I needed for the accountant. We had some time before we needed to go and pick up Jessica. My husband, Randy, decided to go into Portland that afternoon to get some parts for his log truck. He took Brett with him.

When Boone and I returned to the school to pick up Jessica, I could see the excitement on her face. It appeared that her Valentine's Day had been a perfect one.

She hopped in the van, and we headed for Salem, which was a forty-minute drive from our farm. As we traveled, we all sang along to the country music songs that played on the radio. Jessica went through her Valentine folder and showed me all the cards she received that day. She took one Valentine out at a time and read them to me, both the printed messages and the personal messages that went along with them. When she came to one particular Valentine, I remember her saying, "Mom, look what Marianne gave to me. I thought she didn't like me."

"Oh Jessica, that is so sweet," I replied. "See, you thought she didn't like you, but she does. Maybe she just has a hard time showing her feelings for people."

Jessica's look of contentment that day regarding Marianne was unforgettable.

Jessica, with her red curly hair and stunning bright blue eyes, had the heart of an angel. She was known to the kids and teachers at her school as "the peacemaker." If her class-mates were in an argument or if someone fell down at recess, Jessica was always there to help calm the storm.

On our way back from the accountant's office, we were once again listening to the radio and singing together. This time, we even held hands. When we approached the home stretch on Union Mills Road, I turned into our driveway and noticed that the mail had been delivered. Unfortunately, our mailbox was inconveniently located across the road from our house. I pulled to the end of the driveway and asked Jessica if she would get out and get the mail while I sat and waited for her. She didn't want to, but I pleaded with her. I even made a game of it, telling her I would time her to see how fast she could go. She agreed to play the game.

She got out of the van, walked to the edge of the road, looked both ways for traffic (as she always did), and then walked back to the van and said, "Okay Mom, I'm ready!" I looked at my watch and said, "Go!"

My back was to the road as I waited in my van for Jessica to return with the mail. Suddenly, the awful sound of rubber tires screeching, followed by a huge bang, reached my ears. I turned to my right and saw nothing. I turned to my left and saw a car stopped in the middle of the road. A little further down, my daughter lay in the street. My heart started to pound as I opened the van door and ran to Jessica. It wasn't until I approached her body that it registered in my mind that she had been hit while crossing the road.

An elderly gentleman and his wife got out of the car that hit my daughter. The man was grief stricken, hollering and yelling while his wife tried to calm him down.

Jessica was lying on her side in the middle of the road. She did not move at all. Cars approached the scene slowly and drove around Jessica as if nothing mattered to the drivers except reaching their destinations.

My first instinct was to pray. I prayed the same Bible verses I prayed for Boone when he got ran over three years earlier. He ended up being just fine, so I thought that if I said those same prayers for Jessica, she would be okay, too.

While still praying, I ran towards the short line of cars that was now forming along the road, asking anyone if they knew CPR. Not one person knew how to perform the act.

The gravity of what was going on began to overwhelm me. When I approached the last car in line, I asked the driver if she would drive to the gas station at the end of the road. I knew that one of the men there worked for the fire department. He would know what to do.

Returning to comfort my daughter, I could hear the elderly woman tell her husband that there was no use trying to save Jessica, that she was not going to make it. I yelled at the woman, ordering her not to talk like that.

During this whole time, Boone was on the side of the road, wondering what was going on with his sister. As people started to get out of their cars and come to help, I told them to watch Boone as I went inside my house to call 911.

I made the call and then grabbed a blanket on my way back out the door. I wanted to comfort my daughter. As I approached Jessica, I saw that blood was coming out of her mouth and ears. There was not a sign of life in her little body. Her chewing gum was in the middle of a puddle of blood. Her eyes were open and fixed in a distant stare. To this day, the picture is still vivid in my head.

I looked down the road and saw the man from the gas station approaching. Finally, someone was there that could help my daughter. He approached Jessica, and to my dismay, did nothing to try and save her. Instead, he turned to me and told me that she could not be helped. She was already gone.

My immediate thought was *I am not hearing this right.*

The ambulances, fire trucks, police cars, and rescue units came from right and left to assist in a shut down of Union Mills Road. My family came one by one as the news reached them, but my husband was still in Portland, not knowing what had just happened. When my mom and dad arrived, they escorted me into the house to pull me away from the scene and to comfort me as much as they could. The police asked me many questions. One officer after the next, asking me the same questions, again and again. It all felt unreal to me. I could not get the reality of what happened to register in my brain—Jessica was dead!

***

Her body stayed out on the road for hours. The coroner's office was tied up with other deaths. We could not move her body until the coroner came and processed the scene.

During the delay, Randy was on his way home with Brett, still unaware of what happened. As he approached Union Mills Road, he saw that it was blocked off. The detour that the authorities set up made it impossible for him to get home.

He asked a police officer what happened and explained that he needed to pass through the detour to get home. The officer Okayed Randy to drive past the blockade and told my husband that a little girl was hit by a car. Randy's blood ran cold as he drove down the road to our house.

I remember looking at Randy and sobbing as he came through the front door. A sudden fear of losing my husband ran through my mind. I thought he might never forgive me for being the one to ask our daughter to go get the mail.

Randy took me in his arms and we sobbed together. It was all a blur to me.

The house was buzzing with people, and the confusion took its toll on me. I walked into the bathroom to get away from everyone and to try and make sense out of what was going on, but there was no sense to be made. The flood of confusion would not let up. My mind was swimming in circles. My mother found me hiding behind the door. I did not want to come to terms with losing my daughter, my best friend.

Finally, the coroner arrived. He processed the scene and did what he had to do according to the law. Then the police came into the house to tell us they had taken Jessica's body away. The emergency crews and police officers thinned out quickly. Family and close friends were left to comfort one another.

I walked back outside to the road where I had last seen my daughter. I wanted to see if she was really gone or if I was just having a bad dream. *Where did they take my daughter?* I thought. *She can't be by herself. She must be scared.* My thoughts were jumbled. Nothing made any sense.

My parents decided it was best if our family went up to their house to spend the rest of the evening with them. As we left the driveway, my eyes were fixed once again on the place where I had last seen my Jessica.

She wasn't there.

This just can't be, I thought to myself. *There is some-thing wrong going on here. I just spent an awesome day with my daughter. Where is she?*

When we arrived at my parents' house, my father decided to call and ask our minister to come be with us. My mom and sister-in-law thought it would be in my best interest to have a doctor prescribe some sort of tranquilizer to help me get through that night. The doctor and minister showed up at the house at about the same time. I was given a sedative, and within a short amount of time I drifted in and out of reality and into a deep sleep.

An Unwelcome Funeral

CHAPTER 3

I woke up in the wee hours of the morning to the memory of what happened. I forced myself back to sleep so that I wouldn't have to think about it. When I finally got out of bed, my mom was making coffee and breakfast. My mother's presence gave me comfort, and I was content knowing that she and my dad were close by.

Not one of my prayers was being answered as I wanted them to be. Nothing positive from the day before came to my mind. I could not accept the reality of not waking up with my Jessica, not seeing her smile, and not having our normal morning conversation with each other. *Maybe tomorrow she will talk to me,* I thought.

God was in my thoughts, but during this time, all I wanted was for God to give me back my little girl. I wanted things to turn out as they had for Boone during his accident. He was alive and breathing. But my prayers didn't get answered like that, not that day anyway. *I'll try again tomorrow,* I thought.

As morning turned to midday, many phone calls, visitors, and talk of Jessica came my way. My heart was broken, and I was in denial. Our family discussed funeral arrangements. We had to make some decisions: where Jessica was to be buried, what color and type of flowers we wanted on her casket, what type of casket, what day we wanted the funeral, what time. It was too overwhelming for me. I kept searching for answers from God. I seemed to just be floating along, not having too much feeling about anything. There was nothing but pain in my heart and stomach.

Jessica died on a Tuesday. We made the decision to have her funeral that Friday at the Nazarene Church because the building was larger than the Baptist Church we attended. Once we decided on the place for the funeral, we needed to find Jessica's resting place. My parents suggested the Mt. View Cemetery in Oregon City. Relatives from both my mom and dad's side of my family were buried there. We drove to the cemetery and talked with the office people about our daughter passing. We wanted to pick out a spot we thought Jessica would have chosen herself.

We walked through the cemetery and found an area with a plot that had a beautiful view of Mt. Hood. *This is a spot that Jessica would like,* I thought. That area was very peaceful. Near it were some trees that could shade Jessica from the sultry, hot sun in the summer.

My mother and father bought the plot along with four other ones next to it. They did this so that my whole family could be buried alongside Jessica one day. It was like a ray of sunshine beaming down on me to know that one day I would be lying next to my daughter.

From the cemetery, we went to the funeral home where we had to choose a coffin for Jessica. *How will I be able to walk into that funeral home and pick out my daughter's coffin,* I thought. I did not want to do these things. I couldn't even think about the funeral, let alone plan it.

I prayed, "Dear God, please help me through this. I just want to sleep so that I don't have to think."

I had never been to a place where one had to pick out a coffin. It was frightening to me. However, I found the many designs and the many different styles of coffins breathtaking. They were so beautiful. We chose a baby blue coffin lined with a soft blue satin material for Jessica. I knew she would have liked it. We then picked out a funeral announcement that showed a picture of Jesus holding a baby lamb on the front cover.

As I lay in bed that evening, my thoughts turned to God. He, the Maker of all, had my daughter, and I wanted her back! How could I love God through all this when He is the one who took her from me? I was mad at God, and I was a little scared about the fact that I was mad at Him. Who was I to be angry at God Almighty?

"God, help me to deal with all this. I miss my Jessi, and I want her back. I had plans for us. This just can't be happening! Please turn back the time and let me start Valentine's Day over again, PLEASE GOD," I prayed.

Thursday arrived. It was the day the funeral chapel would have Jessica all fixed up for her viewing. Jessica would be wearing an outfit she picked out for herself just weeks before.

It was our mother/daughter tradition to go shopping for a Christmas dress every year. I always had the final word on which dress we purchased, but the Christmas before her accident, I told Jessica she could pick out any dress she wanted, and I would buy it for her. We shopped from store to store before she settled on a black and navy blue checkered satin dress with a big bow in the back. It looked stunning with her red curly hair.

For the viewing, we chose to outfit her in her Christmas dress, along with a golden chain Randy bought her as a gift for Christmas and the black stockings and shoes she wore with the dress.

I anticipated this day because I knew I would get to see my daughter again, and I thought maybe, just maybe, I'd find out that she really didn't die.

When we arrived at the funeral home, we were escorted into a room where she lay in her baby blue coffin. The room was quiet and filled with flowers. The lid to her coffin was open. She was just lying there, so still, so lifeless. I went to touch her on the hand. She was so cold and stiff, it surprised me. I bent down to kiss her on the cheek, and as I did, the feeling of finality was ever so present. I missed my girl, and this just wasn't fair. Nothing was normal about this situation. Little children just don't die. They live to get married and have babies.

My sister and I planned to put our family's pictures inside the coffin with Jessica, so she wasn't by herself. Jessica was always a little scared of the dark, so we thought this would comfort her. I also wanted to put a couple of her favorite stuffed animals in with her. The thought of having familiar things with her inside her coffin, and knowing she wasn't by herself in that box, lifted my spirit.

"God is with you, my little girl. You are not alone," I said to her.

We placed a picture of each family member around the inside of her coffin along with her favorite stuffed animals.

When the day of the funeral arrived, I was eager to see Jessica's friends, our extended family, and our many friends that would come to remember her life. I visualized this gathering as Jessica's last birthday party, a grand finale departure. I wanted to leave an impression in people's minds. My biggest fear was that people would forget about her in future years. I cringed at the thought of no one remembering her.

Our family was in a private room when the church began filling with people. When it was time for the service to begin, our family walked one by one down the aisle to the reserved front pews. As I rounded the corner in the back of the church, my eyes were fixed on Jessica's coffin. It was surrounded by many items: her sports paraphernalia (a soccer ball, her snow skis), her Strawberry Shortcake dolls, her stuffed animals, her picture, balloons, and much more. My heart skipped beats as the realization of what was going on at that particular place and moment struck me.

Please, stop this! I don't want this to happen. I want to rewind the clock and start Tuesday over again, I thought. The physical part of my body seemed to be floating when I saw her coffin, and it got worse when I realized I could not control anything. My feelings were completely numb.

We sat down in the front pews, and the service began. The life of our daughter and how it ended was explained to our guests in the church. Jessica's life, short as it was, was honored that day by everyone attending her funeral. Her life was summed up in one word: love. She had so much love to give. She loved people with the unconditional love that Christ talks about. She was not your typical little girl who just played with dolls and explored. She believed in Jesus Christ as her savior as much as she believed I was her mother. Jessica never doubted Christ's love, and she shared it with others—to adults, to her friends, and to her teachers.

Jessica's teacher, Bob Hageman, was asked by our family to speak at her funeral and shed some light on Jessica's life as he knew it since school started. When Bob reached the podium to talk, his grief overwhelmed him. He stood at the front of the church sobbing, not able to speak. His wife, Susan, came forward and stood by his side to help him through his words. It was evident that Jessica's life made an impact, even on her teacher.

Beautiful songs played during her funeral. The tape of Jessica, Boone, and their cousins singing "Jesus Loves Me," the same tape played at their Great Aunt Geraldine's funeral the month before, also played at Jessica's funeral. Jessica sang at her own funeral. I've thought many times how coincidental it was that the kids taped that song, not knowing it would be played a month later at Jessi's own memorial.

As Jessica's memorial service continued, people stood and gave examples of how she had touched their lives in some way. It was priceless to hear their stories.

After the people left the church, I asked if I could see my daughter one last time. The coffin lid was opened, and I kissed my little girl for the last time. I never saw Jessica's face again.

***

The day after Jessica's funeral, I went to the cemetery to visit with my daughter. Her gravesite was beautiful, overflowing with many flower arrangements. I felt her presence there. I sat and talked to her day after day for weeks thereafter. I didn't want her to feel alone. I told her I would always have fresh flowers for her, and that I would come often to visit with her.

As I grieved the loss of my daughter, I began to write my thoughts about her as letters addressed to her. Not knowing how to deal with my loss or how to grieve, I wrote to her as if I were talking to her.

THE CEMETERY
Jessi,

The cemetery where you're at is a very pretty and beautiful place. There are lots of flowers, green grass that's well cared for, and lots of shade trees. It's a very peaceful place, Jess. Never are there many people around. Your "neighbors" in the ground around you have all died recently. There is a little boy exactly your age, Jessi, about six rows down from you. He also was from Mulino.

I never really know what to do when I come to visit your place. I try to keep busy by watering the many flowers you seem to always have and clearing some long pieces of grass that were missed by the mower. I do always tell you that I love you and miss you. Oh Jess, I miss you so, so much. I long for the day I meet you in heaven. I want so much to hug you for hours and touch your red curls.

I'm so empty, Jessi. You were my closest friend. We shared so much, and I miss that. Your friends are always coming by your "place" and leaving flowers, toys, notes, balloons, and birthday invitations. You are still alive in all our hearts, Jessi. You'll never really die!

Mom

A few days after Jessica was buried, our community got hit by a snowstorm that dumped several inches of snow on the ground. The boys and I thought it was a sign from Jessica to have a day of fun in the snow and to let some "sunshine" into our lives. We went back to the cemetery to share the fun with her, and we made snowmen for Jessica by her tombstone. It was a peaceful day, but one that wasn't normal. Jessica should have been enjoying the snow with us. Nothing was normal, and it was never going to be normal again.

I Can't Move On – I Want to Die

CHAPTER 4

A week had gone by, and the reality of Jessica being gone had yet to sink in. I told myself, "Jessica is gone camping with her friends. She will be back next week." When the next week came and there was still no Jessica, I told myself, "Jessica is gone to church camp this week, but she for sure will be back next week." After a month of these silly mind games, reality hit, and I didn't like it. I missed my daughter. My body ached for her. Grief was ever so present, but I didn't know at the time that it was grief. I thought I was having a nervous breakdown.

I can't adequately explain how my body actually felt as it processed my grief. I was numb, yet I ached from head to toe. I felt a hole in my heart. My arms felt as though bugs were crawling in my veins. I looked forward to going to bed at night because I knew I wouldn't have to think about anything. I wouldn't hurt for a few hours.

After Jessica's funeral, it seemed as if all the days were jumbled together. I didn't care about anything. My life would never be the same.

I reflected on my boys and realized I hadn't had one-on-one contact with them for days after Jessica's death. I had to carry on for the sake of my sons. But how? Life was not good, and it was not easy.

"God, how do I cope with all this?" I prayed.

I recalled the verse I kept close to my heart when Boone had his accident:

> *"No temptation has seized you except what is common to man. And God is faithful; he will not let you be tempted beyond what you can bear. But when you are tempted, he will also provide a way out so that you can stand up under it. (1 Corinthians 10:13)*

I had prayed this verse so many times to God, telling Him that I could not bear to have my son taken from me. At the time of Boone's accident, my burden was lifted as Boone got better. He was alive, and my prayers were answered. The prayer didn't work this time.

Months passed and things weren't getting any better. In fact, they were getting worse. My moods went up and down. I started to argue with Randy. He kept telling me I needed to move on with my life, but I wouldn't listen. His words went in one ear and out the other. Randy was dealing with Jessica's death in a different way than I was. Our separate grieving processes put a strain on our marriage.

From the time of Boone's accident to Jessica's, a three-year span, there was some animosity built up between us. Randy concentrated a lot on his business, wanting more log trucks to expand the company, which required more money. Discontentment developed in my life. I felt that Randy's job was more important than our family (which it was not). I'm not going to give out details, but I will say that Randy and I were developing problems. Our individual responses to losing our daughter strained our marriage to the max.

I started going to a counselor to deal with my feelings. During our sessions, the counselor said something to offend me, so I quit going. I picked a new counselor and started the process all over again. I followed this pattern time and time again. It wasn't the best approach, but each counselor taught me something valuable. They had me focus on my need to talk through my feelings about Jessica's life and death. They said that keeping my feelings inside of me was self-destructive, and I knew it was true. But it was not easy for me to talk about my emotions. I typically kept things bottled up inside of me.

I felt that I was being punished for something in my past, and I didn't want to deal with it. The pain was so intense that I felt I was never going to get better. I knew God had given me friends and family to talk to, but I feared that if I talked about my true feelings to them, they would judge me harshly. So I didn't.

I was advised to start writing a journal of my feelings. This was easy for me to do. I had dabbled in poetry for years as a way to express my feelings. I had kept a journal throughout Boone's ordeal. Once I started my journal, my writing did not stop. My entries were frequently in the form of letters to Jessica.

> *Jess,*
>
> *I just still can't let go of you. I feel better writing like this because I get my feelings out. I do know that you're not here, but yet you're always here. You are with me every minute of every day in my heart.*
>
> *It's been real, real hard for me the last four months. I think the first couple months I was still in a state of shock. I hope I've hit the bottom, Jess, because I don't see how much farther down I could go. I know if you were here and the circumstances were different, you would tell me to get better and that things will be okay. But Jess, it's so hard! I just want to be with you and God. I would be so happy up*

there. Down here there are so many bad things going on. I worry for Boone and Brett, what they will have to go through.

Rudi (our dog) *died Saturday. He was out on the road and got hit by a car. Boone was real sad Jess. All Boone knows is that when someone dies, it's because of a car. You died from a car; Rudi died from a car; Boone was run over by a car. I just sometimes hurt for Boone. He's like me and keeps things pretty much to himself. I try to encourage him to express himself. I pray to God that he will.*

I also have real problems with Daddy and the family. I don't have much to do with them. I don't know why, but I push them away.

Maybe it's because I hurt when I see them and because they don't know what to say to me. Jessi, you know I love them all with all my heart. I just don't know why I do those things to them.

I really wish you were here, but I know where you're at is the best place to be. Sometimes I get jealous of you because of where you are at, and sometimes I get jealous of God because He has you. I long to spend eternity with you and the Trinity.

All my love!

Mom

Spring turned to summer, and my feelings were still not good. No one was telling me how to grieve for my daughter's death other than the counselors I was going to. I felt everyone in my family thought I was going crazy, and maybe I was. Things were getting worse between my husband and me. Our communication was at a standstill, so we decided to start marriage counseling. The more I went to marriage counseling, the more I felt the need to be by myself. I was contemplating divorce.

I blamed myself for Jessica's death. I was the one who told her to go get my mail. She didn't even want to go get it, but I pleaded with her, using a stupid little game of "I'll time you." I felt guilty for losing my child to a stupid game. I felt guilty for breaking her trust. I felt guilty for deceiving her. I just plain felt guilty all the time.

One day, Randy was outside, changing the oil in our van. Boone was with his daddy, trying to help as much as he could. When Randy poured the oil out of the plastic bottle into the motor, the oil was "gulping" out of the bottle and sucking for air. All of a sudden, Boone said, "Daddy, this is what Jessica's stomach looked like when she was lying on the road."

"What are you talking about, Boone?" Randy asked.

Boone responded, "She almost made it across the road!"

It was then that we realized Boone had watched his sister try to cross the road. He saw his sister get hit by the car. He had never mentioned this to us before. His pain had to be unbearable.

After knowing that Boone had witnessed his sister being hit by the car, we decided to take him to some sort of counseling. We heard of a program in the Portland area called the Dougy Center, a place where children could be with other children who experienced the loss of a loved one. This helped him immensely.

August, 1989

When darkness falls, I see no light,
The shadows gone from my sight!
But visions dance within my head,
As I lie down to go to bed.

I dream of things for happiness,
And wish that I was truly blessed.
With a life of love and peace in hand,
Wishing we were playing in the sand.

My feelings come from deep down in,
And I never know just how to begin.
To explain myself when words won't come,
And they look at me as if I were dumb!

So what's wrong with me? I don't know why,
My feelings are gone, and I always cry.
My life's not all here, and it's hard to go on,
Then the next thing I know it's the coming of dawn!

The days go so fast, and the months go by too,
The sun always shines, and the skies are all blue.
So let my heart sing, God, a brand new song,
Because in my heart, I know something is wrong!

Mom

As summer was ending, our church prepared for our fall Bible classes. I taught Jessica's Pioneer Girls class for the last couple years. I enjoyed seeing her with her friends and teaching them about Jesus. I was hesitant about teaching that fall because I wasn't sure I was ready for that. But I wanted to be around Jessi's friends. It made me feel closer to her to be around them. I also wanted to make sure that her friends would not forget her, especially Jennifer, Jessica's best friend.

I kept in contact with Jennifer for my own selfish reasons. I'm not sure how her mother felt about it, but I didn't really care at the time. It was healing for me. Besides, how could she mind when she still had her daughter and I didn't?

1989 - Jessi,

Tonight I went to church to clean my cupboards out for Pioneer Girls. It starts next Wednesday, and I'm going to teach your class again. I just want to be around your friends because we all miss you. Jennifer and Elisha miss you so much. Jennifer still loves you lots. I asked her a while back who her best friend was now. She said, "Jessica." She's a real friend, Jess. Elisha takes real good care of the boys. When we have our gatherings with the family, she just doesn't seem real happy. She gets bored because you're not around to play with her. I love you still, sweetie, and I miss you much.

Mom

I wasn't looking forward to school starting. Jessica *loved* school. She would have entered fourth grade that fall. Boone was entering first grade. I knew when he started school that I would get bored doing nothing. I still had Brett at home with me, but he was going to start preschool. I needed to do something to keep me busy, so I thought about getting a job. If I had a job, my thoughts would be consumed by something other than Jessica.

Jessi,

Well today was Labor Day and tomorrow is the first day of school. Boone is real excited to start first grade. I wish you were here to wait with him for the bus. We went to Taroli's house today for a fish and crab pot luck. Elisha is so sad that you're not here. She misses you so much.

Your tombstone came last Thursday, and it's beautiful. We found another tombstone just like yours, Jessi, but it was a pink heart instead of a black heart like yours. The little girl's name on the tomb-stone was Julie. She was twelve years old. Maybe someday I'll meet her mama. I love ya, Sis, and miss ya. I hope I find a job soon. I'm gonna be bored with Boone in school. I love you!

Mom

I went to Woodburn one day, a neighboring town that's about a twenty minute drive from our house. I drove there to get some fruit for making jam. As I was driving along the country road, thoughts of Jessica flooded my mind once again. I started crying uncontrollably. My feelings were at one of the lowest levels they had ever been. I simply wasn't happy anymore, and I couldn't see the bright side of anything. The depression I was under took a horrible toll on me. I was suicidal.

I remember looking at the telephone poles along the side of the road as I drove and wanting to drive right into one. As I thought about it, it seemed that this was the best solution for me. Then, pictures of my boys' smiling faces came into my thoughts. My crying intensified. I pulled the car over and let the tears flow. What was I thinking? My boys had already suffered so much. They would be lost if someone else they loved were to die.

As I sat on the side of the road, I wondered how long my pain would last? No one ever taught me how to grieve. No one understood what was going on with my body. I cried out to God, "Please help me to deal with this. I am a mess, and I can't do anything. I can't concentrate on anything. I'm not here mentally, and I need help."

I continued to pray on the side of the road until I got my composure. Then I drove back home. As soon as I walked in the door, I took my boys in my arms, hugged them, and kissed them. They were all that was keeping me alive. I needed to make some changes in order to heal. Nothing I was doing so far was working.

***

I started seeing Joann, a Christian counselor who specialized in grief recovery. She lost her husband a few years before Jessica died. Joann was an older woman, maybe in her sixties. I'm not aware of the circumstances of her husband's death, whether it was an illness, natural causes, or a sudden death, but it had a devastating impact on Joann's life. After her tragic loss, she found comfort in helping others with their loss. She wanted to bring good out of her pain, so she started sharing her story with others who had lost someone or something. She helped me understand my grief. She assured me that I wasn't going crazy. I looked forward to seeing her weekly. She related to my pain, and she always made me feel better.

Joann encouraged me to attend a Compassionate Friends meeting where people who have lost a child gathered once a month to discuss their feelings. The first time I went, I was in awe that every single person there had lost a child. I felt connected to people for the first time in a long time. Knowing that other parents in that group felt as I did made me realize that, when someone you love so much dies, you are in shock for a long period of time. It's normal to feel lost. I looked forward to these monthly meetings.

Through these meetings, I learned how God may have felt when Christ died. He understood what it meant to lose a child. The Bible tells us that God loved us so much that he allowed His Son to die for us, so that we might find ourselves through Christ.

"For God so loved the world that he gave his one and only Son, that whoever believes in him shall not perish but have eternal life. For God did not send his

Son into the world to condemn the world, but to save
the world through him." (John 3:16 & 17)

The process of death made sense to me in this manner. I
loved and trusted God, and though I was still angry with God,
I began to believe that maybe He took Jessica to spare her
from some unknown future tragedy. New ways of looking at
her death opened up to me. The grief in me began to slowly
subside.

1989
The summer's almost gone now,
And the weather's been real wet,
We've done our school shopping,
And at last Boone is all set.

I'm pretty sad 'cause you're not here,
You always loved your school,
The reading, writing, and arithmetic,
And never broke the rules.

For Boone, he's all excited,
To start his first full day,
Of sitting in his own desk,
And then at recess out to play.

Then there's your friends, when they see me,
They give me a hug and a kiss,
I think they're really trying to say
How much you're loved and missed.

There's a piece of ground at school,
Where they planted flowers and a tree,
And a plaque with your name on it,
For all the kids to see.

Your teacher, Mr. Hageman,
Has changed in many ways,
I know he loved you very much,
And now I think he prays.

You've meant so much to all of us,
We've all changed in many ways,
I'm just kind of lonely now,
Because it's back to school days.

Mom

Jessica's Miracle to Me

CHAPTER 5

I got a job that I applied for at the Portland Airport. I started it the day before Jessica's birthday. I remember leaving work the first day and crying all the way home. I was so confused. I had no idea what I was doing, but I knew I needed to get a job and move forward with my life. Working was new to me. I had been a stay-at-home mom for ten years. To start a new job while I was grieving wasn't a very good combination, but I had to start doing something.

When I got to work the second day, Jessica's birthday, I confided to one of my coworkers that it was my deceased daughter's birthday, that I was in pain, and that I took the job to take my mind off things. To talk to someone who knew nothing about me or what I had been going through helped to get me through that day.

On my way home I stopped at the cemetery, sat with Jessica at her grave, and told her about what I was doing. I went to the gravesite often and talked to her as if she could hear me. Maybe she could, and maybe she couldn't. I didn't care what anyone thought; it helped me to talk to her.

A few weeks prior, a group of Jessica's friends and their families decided they wanted to erect a memorial at the grade school where she attended. When they approached us with this idea, I was overjoyed.

The area they chose for the memorial was where the children lined up every day to catch the school buses. The memorial formed a large triangle. They planted lots of flowers and a tree in the middle. One of the parents made a memorial centerpiece in the shape of a heart, outlined with iron, and cemented to the ground. In the middle of the centerpiece is a plaque inscribed with: Jessica Jean Noble – Forever Our Valentine 2-14-1989.

I was so overwhelmed by this outward show of affection that I went to visit the memorial many days in a row. Jessica's friends and families were showing us that they would *never* forget her, something I had feared many times would happen. This memorial answered my prayer of keeping Jessica's memory alive forever. Through the coming years, new students and new teachers would ask, "Who is this little girl that is so honored at Mulino School?"

1989 - Jessi,

Today, Brett and I went to Vancouver so that I could have a physical for a job that I got at the airport in Portland. I think I might enjoy this job. I don't need the money; I just need to keep busy, especially since Tuesday is your birthday. I miss you so much, Jessi. I just wish I were with you in heaven. I wish so much that this was December of 1988, when everything was fine and we were all happy. Everything has changed so much. I wonder sometimes if Daddy and I can ever be happy together again. I think we could, but I still have some problems, and it's so hard to deal with them. I drove past the school tonight, and the Greers were down there at your memorial site. Lee made you a beautiful cement heart with a brass plaque on it. It's so pretty, Jessi, and it's yours, for you! You are so missed. The Greers miss you very much, especially Carrie. I went to pick Boone up from school yesterday, and I saw all your classmates playing on the playground. Carrie always comes to me and hugs me. Jennifer usually does, too. Estelle and Brenda sometimes do, and so does Katie. I saw Justin teasing Brenda, and I got a little jealous because I felt he should always like you. Silly, huh? Craiger is always a sweetheart, Jess. He hasn't changed a bit. Miss Drennon wants me to help her class this year, and so does Mrs. Wiegel. I just can't do it, Jess. It hurts me too much. Michelle and Tommy stayed in Mr. Hageman's class again. Michelle gave me a hug yesterday. You and she would have been good friends. Give me strength, Jessi, to go on in this world. I need lots of strength, and I need your love and prayers. I love you, Sis!

Mom

Jessica's memorial dedication was to be held on the evening of her birthday. Earlier that day, while class was in session, I went to the school to check on things before the service. On Jessica's memorial, one of the teachers had tied some balloons. Two of the balloons had all of the pictures from Jessica's third grade class taped to it. They were beautiful.

Later that day, when my mom and I came to pick Boone up from school, the balloons were gone! One of the teachers told me that a gust of wind came through and blew the balloons away. She also said that the principal's wife had come to school just minutes before we got there and said she had seen a batch of balloons floating around her house.

I looked at my mom and said, "Let's go see if those are Jessica's balloons!"

My mom said not to get my hopes up, but I was determined to get those balloons back. I wanted to keep them in Jessica's scrapbook.

We jumped in my mom's car and drove down the road, looking up in the sky for a batch of floating balloons. How ridiculous we must have looked. We turned down the road where the principal lived, about ten miles from the school. I saw no balloons. We drove a little further, and right by his house, were the balloons, floating at the highest point in a patch of fir trees.

We pulled into the driveway, got out of the car, and just looked at each other. "How in the world are we going to get those down from way up there?" I asked.

No sooner had we started discussing this impossible task of trying to retrieve them when a gust of wind suddenly came whisking through. It blew the balloons out of the treetops, and they fell like feathers to the ground, right by the car. My mom and I thanked God for that miracle. We couldn't wait to tell others about what we had just experienced. I still have those balloons to this day.

My mom and I shared stories that day about things that Jessica had done or said that were special to us. My mom shared with me about Jessica being in a Sunday school class that my dad and she taught just before she died. My mother wrote down some memories of Jessica while on a vacation. Here is a portion of one of the letters she wrote:

Jessi,

I wish Grandpa and I would have started teaching Sunday school earlier, as it was so neat to have you in our class. We only got to have you two Sundays while we were teaching. I could tell you wanted to know all about Jesus. You loved Him, and He loved you! The first Sunday, grandpa asked the class, "Who would you like to be like? Anyone in the whole

world!" Everyone had an answer except you, Jessi.
You couldn't think of anyone. You were just happy
being you! That showed God made you special.
The last Sunday we talked about being ready
when the Lord calls us home. In that lesson a seven-
teen-year-old boy dies, and he was ready. Remember
you read the part of the mother who gave the testi-
mony that her son was ready? We didn't realize that
the next Sunday you would be with the Lord and that
you were ready, just like the story we talked about. I
can't tell you, Jessi, how much I loved you and will
miss you.

As our family, relatives, and friends arrived that night
for the dedication, I saw *all* of Jessica's friends and their
parents come to show our family how much they loved and
missed her. There were a couple of musically talented men
from our church that wrote a song for Jessica. They named it
"Jessi." Each word they sang was about my daughter: "She
was loved," "She was missed." Her life touched every person
that was there.

I felt her presence in my heart that night as I listened to
the words spoken of her. My dad spoke at the dedication. He
had a gift for teaching the Bible to others and showing them
the importance of Christ in their lives. As my dad talked of
his granddaughter, it was hard for him at times to speak, but
his words made such a huge impact on the teachers, parents,
and children present that night. Afterward, many people came
up to my father and told him that they wanted to hear more
about Christ. It was a perfect opportunity for our family to
reach out to others and possibly lead them to Christ through
Jessica's death. I saw for the first time that something good
could come from something bad. This gave me hope, the
hope that Jessica's death wasn't in vain.

I prayed to God that He would use her death to reach other people that I had not thought about reaching out to, specifically Mr. Hageman. *But,* I thought, *how could I begin to reach out to anyone when my own life was so messed up?* I prayed that God would provide a way to help me.

September, 1989
Jessi,

Today was another hot day. I'm very tired from working on the ramp with the airplanes. I wanted to write on your birthday, but I was so tired. Your teacher, Bob Hageman, put together a memorial dedication for you at your school. It was beautiful Jess. About 125 people came. Your teacher talked, and then Tim and Jeff from church wrote a song about you, it was absolutely beautiful. Then grandpa talked about you and Jesus. It too was beautiful. You received so many beautiful flowers and balloons. Lots and lots of your friends were there. We all cried because we miss you so. Your memorial plaque was covered with gobs of bouquets and flowers. I know you had a wonderful birthday, Jess. I love you and miss you so much. Pray for me, and talk to Jesus for me, too.

Love Always,
Mom

I was still going to grief and marriage counseling, but things were not getting better between Randy and me. I felt he was not happy with me getting a job. It seemed that whatever I did to help myself was not helping the two of us. I concentrated more on myself than on our marriage. In my mind, I felt the need to help myself before I could help anyone else. The thoughts of a divorce kept entering my mind. When I shared this with some of my family members, they got irritated with me. No one in our family had ever been divorced. In addition to grieving for Jessica, I began to grieve for my marriage.

August, 1989

> *When I look up at the skies, I see a whole new world. I see a beautiful blue, and the higher you look up, the deeper the blue gets. The clouds are so light and fluffy, and the images I see are always a delight. I wonder when I look up, how large heaven really is. I see beyond the blue skies and beyond the galaxies, and then I dream of heaven, God's dwelling place, and what it must really look like. I try to imagine the gates of pearl and the streets of gold and the clear river of the cleanest water ever. Then I envision all the people in the Bible walking and talking with all the people I know who died and believed in Jesus as their Lord. Peace comes to me with a smile as I imagine the sheer peacefulness they all share. How I long to have that one day!*

Mom

Fall settled in. School was going strong. The reality of Jessica being gone forever was clear to me now, more than it had ever been. My body was shrinking. I was losing weight, and my moods went every which way. How long was I going to feel this way? I had been a robot during the past months, just going through the motions. But something inside of me was starting to click. Things were becoming clearer to me.

October, 1989
Jessi,

Well, it's getting close to Halloween once again, and I don't want it to come. You should be here with your brothers and cousins to get candy. Oh Jessi, will this ever get better? I'm so alone in my own grief. I miss you so much. You would be proud of my work, Jess. I can just hear you telling your friends about your mom working with the airplanes. I wish you were here to share that with me. I feel closer to Grandma lately, and I think she is really listening to me and learning of my feelings for the first time and not being so judgmental. Tell Jesus and God I love them, and tell the Holy Spirit to work in my heart. I love ya, Jess.

Mom

Halloween was approaching. My sister and I had always gone trick-or-treating together with our five kids. I was not looking forward to this holiday. I had so many fond memories of spending it with Jessica. But my boys were anxious, so I had to "suck it up" for them. Patti was always there for me during my ups and downs. That night we had our little moment together to acknowledge Jessica before we set out for trick-or-treating.

When the night of Halloween came to an end, I felt relief that one holiday was over. But then I remembered that Thanksgiving and Christmas would soon come, and I did *not* want them to. However, I did enjoy my time with my sister and all our kids that night. The kids brought joy to my life, and I think I even smiled, maybe even laughed, something I hadn't done for a long time.

Halloween Night, 1989

Happy Halloween, Jessi! I'm ready for bed now after a long night of trick-or-treating. Boone was Beetlejuice, and Brett was the Joker. Elisha was a dancer. Theron was a monster. And I, like always, wore my headband with the little bats on top. It wasn't the same without you, Jess. We had a trick-or-treater come to our house. Guess who? Jennifer Henry! It made me smile. Someone stole your white cross with the birthday wreath I made for you. I was real unhappy. I like my job, Jess. I miss you and wish I could share my secrets with someone again, but it wouldn't be the same as it was with us. Good night for now.

I love you!

Mom
P.S. Happy Halloween, my little cheerleader.

"I See Jessi"

CHAPTER 6

Winter was approaching. The warm sunshine days were pretty much gone. They were being replaced by frosty, brisk mornings and cold evenings. One day, while driving with the boys down a country road, I could see the sun trying to come through the mist, leaving imprints of rainbows in the sky. Determined to keep Jessica alive in the boys' minds (especially little Brett's) I told them that whenever they saw a rainbow, to think of it as "Jessica's Slide" in heaven.

On another cloudy day, as the boys and I were driving down the road, Brett burst out with, "I see Jessi! I see Jessi!"

I almost caused a wreck as I swung my head around to see what all the fuss was about.

"What are you talking about, Brett?" I asked.

He looked right at me and said, "I see Jessica, up there."

I pulled the car over to the side of the road and I looked in the sky

"Where, Brett?"

"Right there, Mama. Don't you see her?"

I looked and looked, but I could not see anything where he was pointing. One more time I asked, "Where do you see her, honey?"

He was convinced of what he saw, although I couldn't see anything. I never discouraged him from believing what he thought he saw. Who knows what was there? He was happy the rest of the day. He talked about seeing Jessica in the sky to many of our family members.

1989 - Jessi,

There are little games I play with the boys now that you are gone from us. I do this so that they will always remember you. I tell the boys that a rainbow is your slide in heaven. I even have a bumper sticker that says, "I'm a rainbow hunter." The other game I play is at night, when it's real warm and pretty and the sun goes down and the sky is beautifully colored. I tell the boys that God is letting you paint the sky all your favorite colors. Blue sky, then pink, then purple, then red and orange. The boys always say, "Jessi's painting the sky tonight, Mom." We always think of you. Boone misses you lots, and so does Brett.

Mom

The holidays were approaching. My relationship with my husband seemed to be deteriorating more each day, and I wasn't sure why. The two of us were at odds with each other in our grieving processes, and we just couldn't meet in the middle. I wasn't the best person to be living with at that time. I was hurting, crying, and depressed. It took *all* of my energy on most days to get out of bed. I couldn't think ahead. I just took things as they came.

I kept teaching Jesus to Jessica's friends at church, and it made me feel good to do so. I was doing something positive, and I was keeping Jessica's name alive by mentioning her in our prayers.

1989
Dear Jess,

Hi, Sis! I miss you very much. I realize you're not around here, but I feel a need to write down things that are going on, so I address them to you. I don't care if people think this is wrong. I miss you; therefore, I'll write to you if it makes me feel better. At every Pioneer Girls meeting, you're name is mentioned a lot. Everyone loves and misses you. I found Jennifer's Bible, and she had written "I love Jessica" on the inside cover.

Someone stole your angel that grandma bought you for the tombstone, and someone also stole your white kitty that Sara Fama painted for you for your birthday. It was a terrible thing for someone to do that. I'll always watch over your ground, Jess. I will take real good care of it for you. Love ya bunches.

Mom

One day I heard a knock on our farmhouse door. It was our pastor and another gentleman from our church. I invited them to come in, and Randy came into the kitchen and greeted them as well. As we were sharing some small talk, they asked me how teaching was going with the fourth grade class at church. I told them that I thought things were going well. A few minutes later, I was informed that it would be best if I stepped down from my teaching position, because I was having thoughts of seeking a divorce. They felt I wouldn't be a good example to the kids if I got a divorce. At that time, I hadn't even filed papers for divorce, but rumors had spread. At the time, our church didn't allow divorcees to be placed in any type of leadership. I was completely devastated. I felt this was just one more thing that was turning me away from reality.

I couldn't bear the thought of letting Jessi's friends down, and I felt sure they were all going to forget her. How could this happen? I believed in God, and I felt I was doing what I was supposed to, but now I was being punished for this? How could this be? I ran into the bathroom, shut the door, and cried. I felt the pain of Jessi's death creep back into my broken heart.

Looking back now, it was probably the best thing for me to step down. A big reason I taught the girls was because I wanted them to remember my daughter. The more I thought about it, the more I accepted the fact that this wasn't a good time for me to be teaching anyone. My motives were selfish.

After that episode, I rebelled against God. I was mad at God. I was mad at Him for letting my daughter die, for not saving her like he did Boone. I was mad at Him because I didn't feel good. I was mad at Him because I could no longer be around Jessica's friends at church. I was mad at Him because my marriage was not doing good. I was mad at God for everything. I blamed God for all my unhappiness and not myself. I didn't want to feel any more guilt in my life.

I quit going to church for a spell. I decided to do my own thing. Although, I did let my parents take my boys to church. I felt it was important not to disrupt their lives because of my problems. During this time, I wasn't talking to my family much. They didn't want me to get a divorce, so I felt as though they were pressuring me to make my marriage work no matter what.

When things were too much for me to handle, I learned to put up a "big wall" in my head. I trained myself how to shut out my feelings. If I didn't know how to handle or deal with a certain situation, I would put up the big wall. If thoughts of

Jessica made it hard for me to carry on, I put up the big wall. If thoughts about wanting a divorce were getting to me, I put up the big wall. If my family was trying to talk me out of getting a divorce, I put up the big wall. I just simply couldn't handle what life had dealt me, so I ignored my feelings.

1989

Jess,

Tonight, Dad took the boys to a football game in Oregon City with the Taroli's. I stayed home to rest because I work tomorrow. Boone has a soccer game tomorrow. He is real good friends with Eric, Issac's brother. You would be so proud of Boone and Brett. They're growing up so fast.

I feel like I'll be seeing you soon, Jess. This world is so awful. I think God will come soon (at least I hope so). I love you and miss ya lots.

Mom

Life went by slowly for me. I was working and trying to get a routine back in my life. My workdays normally started at four in the morning. This put the burden on Randy to take the boys to the babysitter's. Between my mother and a couple of regular babysitters, the boys were well looked after. I got off work at noon, so I was able to pick the boys up at a decent time and spend some quality time with them in the afternoon. I went to bed early at night, and then started the routine all over again the next morning. All the while, I still attended my counseling sessions.

Through counseling, I learned to stand up for myself. I was able to discuss my feelings with my husband and family. Getting certain issues off my chest helped me to heal, but it put a wedge between me and those I loved. I was to the point that I didn't care who I hurt. I had to look after myself. No one else knew what I was going through.

I still ached daily for my daughter. I still cried. I still hurt inside and felt that empty hole in my heart. I didn't know if it would ever get filled again.

1989 - Jessi,
I don't know what to do,
I just miss you!
The pains come and go,
And the tears seem to always flow.
At times I sit on your bed
Or lie down with your pillow on my head.
I look up at your canopy, and I see your precious kitty posters on the wall. Then I wonder why God would allow such a depressing thing happen to me, taking my most precious friend in the whole world away from me? It's still hard to believe I won't ever see you again, but the Bible says we will one day see each other in heaven. The lady at this grief counseling says that we need to learn how to live now, and that you're not a part of our lives anymore. That's hogwash, Sis! I don't care what they say, you are, were, and ALWAYS will be a big part of my life. I love you, and I know you loved me!

Mom

Going back to a few years earlier to when Boone was hospitalized, I remember looking out the third story hospital window at the freeway and watching the cars and trucks buzzing by early in the morning. I thought to myself, *How can this world continue to go on when my world is falling apart? No one knows the pain I am feeling. No one knows that my child may not live. How can they be so cold to not care about me?* Those thoughts would come into my mind often as I was reaching out to find any answers to why so many bad things happened to me. In reality, I was searching for the answers that I taught Jessica's friends in Bible class. I was searching for God's love and not realizing it. I was too stubborn to open my heart and mind to find the answers sitting right there in the Bible. I had to endure the pain and suffering to know how and where to find my peace. But I wouldn't find it in the near future. I still had some suffering yet to do.

> *Sis,*
>
> *Hi honey! Tomorrow is Thanksgiving, and I'm not in the mood for the holidays. I'm not real "thankful" for this year, Sis. I'm not looking forward to Christmas, either. My life will never be the same again without you, but I will try for the boys. I know happiness is out there. I just need to look. I love you from the bottom of my heart.*
>
> *Mom*

Thanksgiving was upon us, and my thoughts of divorce were pretty final. I didn't want to file until after the holiday season, though. I didn't want to wreck the season for my boys. When Thanksgiving came, I did not want to go to my parents' house and celebrate with a big turkey. I had nothing to be thankful for. I was still mad at God, and I wasn't getting along with my family. But I wanted my boys to share in the love they all gave to them, so I put up my big wall and pretended it was just another day.

At dinner, my father asked each of us to say at least one thing we had to be thankful for. "Oh dear God, help me to get through this," I prayed. As I listened to my family one by one, they each brought up Jessica's name and remembered something special about her. This was healing for me, but very emotional. They all missed her as much as I did.

At this point, I started sharing some of my feelings with my sister, just little things that I needed someone other than a counselor to talk about with. No one in my family really knew what was going on in my life outside of what my husband told them. I finally decided to take a step and reach out to them. I talked more openly about what I was feeling.

Thanksgiving ended up being a good day for me. It was hard to get through the holidays that first year after Jessica's death. Jessica loved the food, and she always looked forward to Thanksgiving— especially the time when we shared what we were thankful for. I could still see her in my mind, sitting there amongst us. As we all talked about her around the table, part of her really was there. Part of her always will be.

The Ultimate Christmas Gift

CHAPTER 7

My relationship with my family started to mend. During the winter months my dad and I decided to have a Bible study. There were lots of people that had kept in touch with me since Jessi's funeral, and they always asked how I was doing and if there was anything they could do for me. So I asked my dad if he would be interested in leading a Bible study once a week for some friends of mine. Of course he agreed to this.

Jessica's teacher, Bob Hageman, the one whom she thought might be an atheist, decided to come. I think he attended at first only to comfort me. His wife had been a born-again Christian for many years, and she prayed for her husband many times to seek God's love and way of life. Week after week, Bob and his wife came. We started seeing a positive change in him. He asked questions, hard questions. My dad always had an answer for him. I believe Bob understood in his heart the teachings of God, but the distractions of the world had a better hold on him. He was having a battle within himself.

Finally, one night, he surprised us by telling our group that he had accepted Jesus Christ as his personal savior. He said it was because of a little redheaded, nine-year-old girl who showed him love in his classroom. Jessica's life had made a big impact on her teacher. Something good came out of her death. Jessica would have been so happy to know that her teacher acknowledged Jesus Christ as his savior. Our family was so pleased to hear of his decision. It was the ultimate Christmas gift.

Bob wrote a brief summary of his life dating up to Jessica's death. Here is his story:

"Jessica"
By Bob Hageman

Life was something I always enjoyed. Following high school, I'd gone in the army. After that I "bummed" around California for several years. Usually I worked, but having fun was more important to me. I lost more than one job because of my priorities.

When that lifestyle became old, and I knew I should get serious about my future, I began going to college on a more full time basis. By this time, I had moved to Portland, Oregon. I met a lovely girl, but I was in no hurry to marry. As time went on, I realized this, too, was something good that would add to the happiness in my life. So after dating a little over a year, we were married.

We enjoyed each other and our first years together. Soon after we married, I completed my college degree and began teaching in a small town south of Portland.

Throughout all these years, I knew God existed, but I had no relationship with Him. I would often say I was an atheist. That sounded like the "in" thing to say.

After a few years, we started our family. Two daughters came quite quickly—the first by adoption, followed six months later by a natural child. These were fun years, too, as we watched the girls grow.

Church was for my wife and daughters. Maybe I'd go on Christmas and Easter, or a special program. Many years went by this way.

When life wasn't going the way I wanted, I would do something to change it. I had been teaching sixth through eighth graders for sixteen years. Each year, they were becoming harder and harder to deal with. I transferred to the primary school and began teaching third graders. I had heard that these children actually liked their teachers, and I was finding that it was mostly true. As the saying goes, "I felt like I had died and gone to heaven."

As time went by and the children became individuals, Jessica stood out! She was always happy and caring. All the other children seemed to be drawn to her. New students felt so welcome and at home because of Jessica.

She was so nice to everyone. I could count on her to help me in many ways. Her sticker chart always had the most stickers!

Often, I would comment to my wife about Jessica. It was hard to believe a child could be so perfect.

Teaching third grade really put my enthusiasm back in teaching. Jessica added to that enthusiasm. The school year was going so well. In fact, it was flying by.

Valentine's Day is always special for the children. We had a good day at school, with a party in the afternoon. Several of the children brought me small gifts. Jessica gave me a can of Almond Roca.

About six o'clock that evening, we were eating a light dinner (after too much candy all day) when the phone rang. One of the other teachers called to tell me that Jessica had been hit by a car and killed. Dinner was left uneaten. This was a shock that I had never experienced before. I knew how much I hurt; how could her family possibly deal with this?

My wife held me, and we sat on the daveno. The phone continually rang, teachers and others calling me. I began calling my students' parents so that they could tell their children in the best way they could. This evening was the hardest I had ever been through.

It had been quiet for a while when the phone rang again about 8:30 PM. I could not believe it. It was Jessica's mother! How could she possibly be able to call me at a time like this? She told me how much Jessica loved me and that I was her favorite teacher. All I could say was, "Lori, I'm so sorry. I'm so sorry." Tears were streaming down my face.

I was asked to say a little about Jessica at her funeral. I worked very hard on what I would say. It had to be just right. Finally, I said to my wife, "I want to end it by saying I know she is safe in the arms of Jesus, but I don't want to be hypocritical."

"I think you know that it is true," my wife said.

Slowly I nodded my head "yes."

Christmas approached fast, and my work kept me busy. I finally talked to a lawyer about getting a divorce, but I still wanted to wait until after Christmas. There were many times that my heart ached for Randy, but for some reason I just couldn't seem to connect with him. I totally tossed aside all feelings regarding my marriage. In my mind there was no chance for its survival. I gave up on it completely.

Unlike me, my boys eagerly anticipated the approach of Christmas. They were growing up fast. Boone was the oldest child now. He started watching over his brother much in the same way that Jessica watched over him. Their brotherly love became a best friend relationship.

December, 1989
Dear Jessi,

Hi, Jess. Yes, I'm still sad for you. I wish with all my heart you were here. I think you were happy here. I hope you were. Jessi, since I was your age, I always dreamed of having my own little girl to love me and share things with me. You fulfilled my dream. I just wish it could have lasted longer. I'm so sorry for any insecurity you may have had. I loved you very much. I will get through Christmas this year, but only for the boys. I miss ya, Sis, so much still. You are still so loved and missed down here by family and friends. Jennifer loves you so much, I can't wait to see you again, and the same goes for Elisha. Gotta go, babe. I love you!

Mom

Christmas Eve was when our family celebrated Christmas together. December 25 was my birthday, and my mother always separated my birthday from Christmas to make me feel special. Brett's birthday was on December 23, and my sister's birthday was on January 1. So our family had several special holidays to celebrate within a one-week timeframe.

Through all the counseling I had gone through, each counselor agreed that, when someone is grieving, the holidays are the hardest times of all for them to endure. I didn't want to go to family gatherings. They made me hurt, and I was tired of hurting. I needed strength to go on. "God, where is my strength?"

Oh Jessi, Oh Jessi, how can it be
That you have departed away from me?
My life it feels so incomplete,
As I felt the last of your little heart beat.
I seem so lost, and I feel half dead,
As I'll never again see your precious head!

I filed for divorce right after the New Year began. Our divorce was not a simple one, but we got through it. The main thing we both agreed on was the well-being of our boys. Randy and I kept in close contact with each other, and it helped the boys to know they would see each of us every other weekend. It took some time getting used to not having the boys in my life every day. During their times away, I sometimes felt that I had lost all my children. But I talked to the boys often on the days I didn't have them, and they got used to going back and forth. They were aware that something needed to be different in their parents' lives. We tried to make them comfortable in knowing that we were both always there for them, no matter what, and that they were our number one priority. They told each of us how much they loved us when they were with us. They knew how much both of us were hurting. Both our boys were very compassionate, and they still are to this day. This arrangement worked out for several years, until the boys graduated from high school. During the times the boys were gone, I felt I could concentrate on myself, something I had not been able to do since I had children.

During this time I focused on getting God back in my life. I needed to have peace in my life again, but I wasn't sure if I could let my guard down. I feared that something else bad was going to happen. I needed to be prepared at all times for something bad to happen. I had no control over this feeling. Tragedy happened twice to me now. The only child that nothing bad had happened to was Brett. I became overly protective in an attempt to guard myself, my feelings, and my children. As the boys grew older, I made it a point to always know what they were doing or where they were going. If they were doing something that looked dangerous (as boys often do), I would throw a hissie fit to remind them that they shouldn't do such things, someone could get hurt. In their high school years, if they were driving somewhere or going to a function, I *had* to know what time they would be back. If they were five minutes late, I panicked. It was a fear I had no control over.

January, 1990

She loved so much to ever be forgotten,
And my love to her was spoiled rotten.
Her eyes were as blue as the sky above,
And she flew to heaven like God's white dove.

Her lips were as red as a perfect rose,
And she had the cutest little button nose.
Those locks of hair were of curls in red,
That fit so perfectly on her blessed head.

Her heart was of gold, for she'd give and she'd give,
Now her life is complete, for she'll live and she'll live.
I love you, Jessi, forever and beyond,
For my love for you is so very fond.

The day when we meet, I can't wait to embrace,
For I'll see you coming, and you'll win the race.
Meet me at those gates of pearls,
So once again I can see those red curls.

I love you, Jessi, and I always will,
Look down at me, at my window sill.
I'll blow you a kiss, so catch it up there,
You know I love you, and you know I care.
Love, mom

Valentine's Day and the one-year anniversary of Jessica's death were at hand. My moods were getting to me again. I relived the memories of the accident in my mind. I was thinking day and night about Jessica. I was thinking about the accident. I was thinking about my divorce. I was thinking how much my life had changed within one year. Up went my big wall again, and that worked for me through Valentine's Day. My family was very supportive of me during this time. Many good thoughts of Jessica were alive. I was happy that people still loved and missed her.

Thoughts about Jessica and why she was not with me haunted me. I wanted justification for why she died. I wanted to know if the man who hit her was speeding. I wanted to know about this man and why he didn't avoid hitting her.

I had asked one of my coworkers if he would come with me to the sheriff's office. I wanted to talk to someone who could answer my questions. We were welcomed into the sheriff's office and taken into a room to wait while they pulled Jessica's file. When the detective came in, he started telling me what her injuries were. I stopped him. I didn't want to know this. I never even wanted her to have an autopsy, as I knew I would dwell on her injuries. I simply wanted to know if the man who was driving was at fault. I wanted to blame someone for losing my daughter. I wanted to blame someone for my life falling apart. I wanted answers. The detective told me that the man was not speeding and that my daughter made a mistake when she didn't look the second time before she went to cross the road. I left the sheriff's office with the weight of blame still resting on my shoulders.

Life Goes On

CHAPTER 8

A few months after Jessica's death anniversary, I realized that there was no one to blame for what happened. I needed to let go and stop blaming myself for her death. I grew to accept that God wasn't the cause of her death, either. I blamed Him for a long time for allowing this to happen, as it was easier to blame Him than to blame myself. It was painful for me to accept her being gone forever. I felt I should have been able to prevent her death from happening. But all the counseling I went to helped me to accept that accidents are accidents. If we knew when an accident was going to happen, we would prevent it. But we don't know the future.

I struggled with life for a long time. I had my good days and my bad days. I was living on the farm still and earning a little over minimum wage at the airport. Before Randy and I divorced, we were buying our farm from my parents. During the divorce, we gave it back to them. I then began to rent it from them. The farm was an awesome place to raise two boys. We had eighteen acres with a large creek running through the back of the property. The boys and I camped down at the creek in the summer, played in the water, sat around the campfire at night, and had fun. I tried to get a grip on "normality" for my boys' sake. I wanted to make fun memories for them. We learned to live life without Jessica, but she was talked about almost daily for several years. She was never far from our thoughts.

Many times I wondered where I would find the money to buy the things my boys needed, but my parents always came through when they needed clothes or something special for sports or school. I worked very hard to get my life back on track. I wanted to be self-sufficient, buying my children the things they needed instead of depending on help from others, and I did. I worked my way up the ladder at my job, and I was promoted to an office position where they taught me how to do payroll and billing. This brought a welcome raise in pay that was an answer to my prayers.

As the first few years after the accident passed, each holiday was devastating to me. I would always remember my child that should be sitting with us at Thanksgiving dinner and opening presents at Christmas. I would remember the little traditional sayings or things that Jessica would always do during a particular holiday. I did not enjoy holidays for probably the first three years after her death.

Boone came through his sister's accident pretty well. We were quite worried about him the first couple years, knowing he watched her get hit. With the problems he had suffered from his own accident, we felt it might be too much for him to handle. But after being counseled at the Dougy Center for a short time, he adapted well to all that had happened.

We tried very hard to keep Jessica's name spoken so that Brett would not forget her. He was only three years old at the time of her death. We wanted to keep her in his thoughts. Brett has some memories of her, triggered mostly when pictures of her are shown to him.

As the boys grew older and were entering junior high and high school, our lives were going smoothly. Randy and I were communicating much better for the sake of the boys and this made life much easier for them. Sports for each of them were important. Life seemed to be going its course.

I did all I could to give my boys a normal life, considering all the turmoil we had gone through. I felt I was doing the best I could, being a single mother, to keep them happy.

My thoughts and pains for Jessica were always near. Not a day went by that I didn't think of her. I regained control in my life by learning how to deal with my many roller-coaster days. I wrote my final letter to Jessica around the time of what would have been her eleventh birthday.

September, 1990
Dear Jessi,

Hi honey! Well, it's been almost a year since I've started work. I like my job, but I don't get paid very well. It's almost your birthday again, and I'm doing a lot of thinking about you. Last night I cried in my bed for you because I miss you still so much.

I can still remember your soft little lips and how you would pucker up like Shirley Temple to give kisses. I love you, Jessi, and I'm so glad that you don't have to experience any more pain here on earth. Daddy and I are divorced now, but we still love the boys very much. Boone and Brett still talk of you a lot and they always will. Everyone misses you so, but not like I do, Sis.

There's a part inside me, Sis, a pain in my heart and gut that never goes away, a little empty feeling. It will never be filled. I love you so much, and I miss you. You're in my thoughts every hour still, Jess, everyday.

I love you!

Mom XOXO

As of this writing, it has been eighteen years since my daughter passed away. I've had many ups and downs, but I have finally found peace within myself once again. More importantly, my love for Jesus Christ has been restored. I have accepted what happened to my daughter, and through years of grieving, my unexplainable fears have subsided. My trust in God remains and it will never be shaken.

Understanding Grief

CHAPTER 9

S everal times during my time of grieving, I dwelt on things that I regretted saying or doing to Jessica as she grew up. I would get so depressed over these thoughts. My counselors explained to me that everyone in my situation goes through this thought process. Through those experiences, we are being developed into the person who we are. It showed me that no one is perfect except Christ Himself.

Parents that I've talked to who have lost a child shared these same feelings of regrets and the "what if" we could have done something differently. Now that I am an "experienced" griever, I can share my feelings with others.

Jesus Christ has helped me more than anyone or anything that I came in contact with during my years of grief. It took me several years to realize that God was hurting along with me. I was too busy blaming God for everything to let Him remove my own feelings of guilt.

I've become a compassionate person to those who are grieving a loss, especially if it is the loss of a child. I want to comfort them if they will let me by sharing what I have gone through. I want them to know that the feelings they are experiencing are normal. Our society does not openly talk about death and grief because they are unpleasant things to talk about, yet they are very natural thing's that happen.

I've learned through my experience that no two people grieve the same way. Jessica's father and I grieved in different ways, and it caused us to argue. He felt I should get on with my life, and I resented that. As I look back now, I believe he was trying to tell me that we could get through it, and that I needed to try harder. But I couldn't. I felt he was going on with his life more easily than I was; therefore, I felt he wasn't as bothered by her death as I was. That was wrong thinking. The counseling we went to at that time was okay, but I should have waited longer and encountered more of it before I made some of the decisions I made.

I remember one time, not too long after Jessica was gone, I was shopping in the grocery store. When I came to the cereal aisle, I started crying when I saw Jessica's favorite cereal. I was devastated because my "normal" was not normal anymore. I saw a friend of mine coming around the corner with her cart. When she saw me, she backed her cart up and went down the next aisle. Why? Later, she told me she didn't know what to say to me. At the time, I felt that no one liked me, that they all blamed me for my daughter's death. Moments like the one I just described strengthened those negative feelings.

People need to know that when someone's child dies, the living parents are in shock, full of anger, looking for answers to why the death happened. They look to blame someone for their loss and for anything to help ease their pain. When someone you know loses a child, you do not have to say anything to comfort them. Just reach your hand out or take them in your arms, give them a hug, and tell them you love them and that you are sorry for their loss. That's all you need to do.

A friend of my mother's had a son that flew an airplane. Before Jessica's accident, his plane crashed at a local airport.

He died in the crash. One day, my mother brought her friend to my house, thinking it might be good for me to talk to her. As we were talking, I could tell her grief was still overwhelming, and her son had been gone for a couple of years already. Her responses to me were, "It's going to be a long, long time before you get the energy to do anything" and "The pain you will endure for the months ahead will seem unbearable" and "Nothing you do can comfort you during this time." By the time this lady left, I felt so depressed that I never wanted to see her again. I decided to never say such things to someone else if his or her child died. People need people when death occurs. Just remember that it is better to say nothing at all instead of saying something that will slow a person's ability to accept loss. Don't ignore a grieving person. They need your love. They need your support. And most importantly, they need to know that you are there for them.

I recently had a friend who lost her son. He was one of Brett's best friends. Nick was twenty years old and in the prime of his life. He was hit by a car while visiting his sister in Arizona. My friend is still deeply grieving the loss of her son, and my heart simply breaks to know the pain and suffering she is going through. When I talk to my friend, I am very careful about what I say to her. I want to let her talk freely, and I want her to process all the emotions that are brought on by grief: shock, numbness, denial, and disbelief, followed sometime later by guilt, anger, loneliness, despair, sadness, and regret. This is the normal progression when walking through grief.

As I see my girlfriend grieving, it is like a mirror of the pain I once endured. This mirror shows me how far I have come and how God can now use me to comfort others.

Grief can last for months or years. If you are grieving, don't ever let anyone tell you that you need to get on with your life. They have no clue what you are going through.

I know it hurts. I know its gut wrenching and it feels like you can't go on. But I am here to tell you that YOU WILL SURVIVE, YOU WILL GET THROUGH THIS and YOU WILL GO ON WITH YOUR LIFE WHEN YOU ARE READY. It just goes by slowly.

Also, if you are grieving, don't make any life changes in the early stages of your grief. When Jessi died and my divorce was in full swing, I wanted to just pack up and move to a different town. I thought it would be a quick fix to ease my pain. Family and counselors encouraged me to not make such a life-changing decision. Most people who do so only delay the grieving process. If I had moved, it wouldn't have helped. I would have fallen back at some point to where I was originally.

After many, many years of not having my daughter around, I have moved on. But the loss is still very near to me. I am happy, smiling, and laughing again, though at one time I thought I would never be able to enjoy life, ever! I remember the first time I actually laughed out loud after Jessica died. I felt as if I were not being faithful to her, when in fact I was being true to myself. That laugh showed me that life goes on, even though bad things may still continue to happen.

God has given me the ability to share His love and to be there for others. I don't know why bad things happen to good people, but I do know that time is the best healer. It's just that time seems to go by so slowly, and we have to experience the heartache and the pain that we don't want to deal with. It hurts. It's gut wrenching. It's not supposed to happen. Parents are supposed to die before their children do. But time heals your body and your heart. And most importantly, God will help you get through this time if you let Him. In my case, I knew my daughter was in the presence of God, the most desirable place to be. Someday, we'll be together!

"My Sweet Jessi"

Baby Jessi, little one,
How you brought me so much fun!
A girl, I prayed with all my heart,
God gave me you, for a start.
Your eyes of blue and hair of red,
Your quiet spirit as you lay in bed.
You were the apple of my eye,
I never dreamed I'd say good-bye!

Little Jessi, Little girl,
Beautiful smile and long red curls.
You grew so fast, no baby no more,
You stole our hearts and were so adored.
Our talks of Jesus and your faith in Him,

Never a doubt and your heart never dim.
You always played with your baby doll,
And hung close to Mommy in shopping malls.

Little Jessi, Little gal,
You were my best friend, my little pal!
They called you the "Peacemaker" when friends were down,
You made them smile and spread love around.
You watched over the boys, just like a mother,
You were the big sister, and like no other.
You liked my friend's gossip, and sat in with us,
I shared you my secrets that were hard to discuss.

Little Jessi, Little lady,
You always were a little "afraidy."
You didn't like storms, and you didn't like strife,
But you would have made someone a wonderful wife.
I don't know why things sometimes go wrong,
But I know I miss you since you've been gone.
When we meet up in heaven, I will understand.
Why God took you away, as we walk hand in hand.

Little Jessi, Little Jess,
I love you still and may God bless.
I think of you every single day,
And sometimes wonder why you went away.
As my life goes on, you are my guide,
You and Jesus on each of my sides.
Happy Valentine's Day, Sis, I love you dear,
And oh how my heart wishes you were here.
Love, Mom

If you have experienced a death of a child, you are not alone. You will get through this most horrible time of your life. Take each hour as it comes. Don't make future plans. You will have a tendency to change your mind often, depending on your feelings during any particular hour. Your feelings change by the minute, and you might think you are going crazy, but you're not. Its grief! Look to family and friends to talk to. Find at least one person in whom you can confide (Jesus Christ is my suggestion). God loves you and wants to comfort you, so let Him!

There is no right way to grieve—you just do it. When you see someone grieving, give them a hug, a handshake, or just say nothing and listen to them. Tell them you love them if you can't think of anything to say. Don't tell them you understand, because you don't. Don't tell them it was God's will, because in their eyes it isn't. Don't tell them that it will be all right, because it is not all right. Don't tell them to call you if they need anything; they won't. Just hug them, tell them you love them, and listen to them.

My love goes out to those whose hearts are aching and breaking. I *do* know how you feel and I *do* know the pain and emptiness in your heart. There is hope, just hang on and depend on Christ to help you through this.

Valentine's Day, of course, is never the same for me. These eighteen years since Jessica has died I have missed having a girl in my life. No one has come close to filling the space she left behind. I look forward to the day when Boone and Brett have special gals in their lives. Maybe I can become close to their wives and have two special girls in my life. Jessica is still in my heart, and I must admit there are days now that go by when I don't think of her, but it's not that I don't miss her. It is just life. When Valentine's Day comes, love your family as if it were the last time you could see them. Tell them you love them. God bless you!

And they brought young children to him, that he should touch them; and his disciples rebuked those that brought them. But when Jesus saw it, he was

*much displeased, and said unto them, "Suffer the
little children to come unto me, and forbid them not;
for of such is the kingdom of God. Verily I say unto
you, Whosoever shall not receive the kingdom of
God as a little Child he shall not enter therein."
And he took them up in his arms, put his hands upon
them, and blessed them.
(Mark 10:13-16)*

This picture was drawn by Jessica.
I found it on the inside cover of her Bible.

In 1989, when you went away,
On that very Valentine's Day.
I knew you would be happy where you are,
Which is above the clouds and stars.

That day will soon come,
When God will take his Christian ones.
He will lift them like a feather,
And me and you will once again be together.
Boone Noble
(Jessica's brother)

Lori's Story
MADE WHOLE BY GOD

"A New Phase of Life"

CHAPTER 1

After seven years of being single, I started dating again. I felt a peace about the idea of being in a relationship, should the right man come along. I went on some dates with a few different men, but none stuck. It was a man from my past who captured my heart.

One October evening, I went to a local restaurant to get a bite to eat. When I walked into the building I saw John, an old friend my brother used to run around with in his twenties. When our eyes met, he asked me if I would like to sit down and join him. As we conversed about my family and friends from our past, I was caught off guard. I realized I was enjoying his company.

John is a real woodsman—stout, strong, and tall. He had worked cutting trees for both my father and my brother at times. I felt safe being around him, and I knew that he would protect me if need be. His big blue eyes and prematurely silvered hair were attractive to me. We met often, and our relationship flourished.

My boys were great around John. They immediately liked him. When they saw how happy he made me, they wanted him to stick around more. They hadn't seen me happy like that in years.

After a couple years of dating, we decided to get married. We tied the knot on December 31, 1996. On that day, I took on the new roles of stepmother and grandmother.

John has two girls from a previous marriage. Megan, his youngest, was in college when we got married. She is now married to Jack. Together, they have a little girl, Kylie Mae, and a baby boy, Brady Dean. Dawn, John's oldest, was already married when John and I wed. She and her husband, Todd, have two adolescent sons, Alex and Erik. All of our children and grandchildren get along well.

My boys were in middle school when John and I married. Jessica had been gone for many years, but I still thought about her a lot. As time passed, so did the pain. Since being married to John, I've found myself enjoying life in a way I never thought I could again.

In 1997, John and I decided to purchase the farm I had been renting from my folks. It was around then that I decided to leave my job at the Portland Airport. One of my former co-workers told me about a job opening at a major janitorial company in Portland. It paid considerably more than what I was making. I made contact with this company, and they hired me to inspect the work of their janitors and to make sure our clients were pleased with our services. This job was a breath of fresh air for me. I was able to get out of the office daily to travel and meet new people.

I stuck with the job for four years before I grew weary of the daily commute. I would travel sixty miles to and from work each day, not including the miles I had to drive to inspect my buildings. After working in Portland for nearly eleven years, I had my fill of overcrowded highways and road rage. I started looking for a job closer to home.

I was hired for a management position in my hometown, Molalla. I gave my notice at the janitorial company and moved on. I was employed at this job for a little over two years before I was laid off due to downsizing. I found myself unemployed for the first time since I started working after Jessica's death.

I spent the next year and a half working around the house and looking for the perfect job. I wanted to make sure I found a job that would bring me contentment. The thought of working with kids kept entering my mind. All my life, I have been blessed with the ability to communicate well with children. It didn't matter what age they were, I was always able to communicate on their level. I thought that a job working with kids would be perfect for me.

A friend of mine who drove a school bus told me her employer was hiring. I put in an application and got the job. Thus began my new occupation as a school bus driver.

Brett was a senior in high school during my first year of driving bus. He was the only person who wasn't happy about my new job. He thought I was spying on him. Regardless, he was a big help. If I had a problem with a kid on my bus, I would tell Brett to meet me where the buses loaded so that I could point out my problem child to him. He would give the problem child his "mean" look, let him know I was his mom, and told them not to mess with me. It worked. Overall, my kids were great.

A couple years went by, and I settled into driving a regular route: Route 8. I drove kids of all ages, from kindergarten through twelfth grade. My route required me to drive on old country roads and well traveled highways. The only part about the job I didn't like was dealing with drivers who ignored my blinking red lights and passed me when I stopped to pick up or drop off kids.

Boone and Brett remained close as brothers and friends. After Brett graduated from high school, he moved out of our house right away, something most eighteen year olds seem to have to do to prove their independence. Boone, who had been graduated from high school for three years, stayed home. He was working full time at a local lumber mill during the day and going to ITT Technical Institute in Portland in the evenings. Boone had thought about moving out to be on his own, but John and I talked him into staying at home to save money while he went to school. Brett was not interested at all in attending college.

John and I had been attending a local church in Molalla for approximately two years when problems arose and our minister was let go. We decided to go back to the church where I first came to know the Lord, the Molalla Conservative Baptist Church, now called Grace Church. When we first attended, we felt very much at home and welcomed by many friends from our past. We've been there ever since.

In 2005, my parents decided to put their house on the market. It was a beautiful home that sat adjacent to our property. It rested on ninety acres of land, was separated from our property by Milk Creek, and had a spectacular view. Eventually, a couple fell in love with their estate and placed an offer on it.

In the meantime Boone was preparing for his last semester of college and looking for a job in his trade. He was offered a two-year contract through FEI at Micron in Boise, Idaho. This was a big deal for Boone. He had never lived on his own before. Taking this job would force him to move several hours away. He prayed about it and made the decision to take the offer.

With all of my family moving, John and I decided to sell our farm. We jokingly said that the same people buying my folks home might want to buy our place for their hired hand. We listed our farm, and ironically, the couple buying my parents' home placed an offer on it, too.

We closed the sale in September of 2006. Due to some delays on the buyer's end, they agreed to give us until the end of the year to move out. We had no idea how significant that extra time would become.

In a Twinkle of an Eye

CHAPTER 2

In October, we found a house we liked just four miles down the road on a half-acre lot within the city limits of Molalla. It had a big shop out back and was all fenced in, which was perfect for the dogs. It was a 70s ranch-style house, about half the size of our farmhouse. It was just right for the two of us.

We wanted to make some changes inside the house, so we hired a contractor who was able to start at once. He finished just before Thanksgiving, leaving us the dreaded task of moving all of our stuff.

Living in one house for twenty-five years, I accumulated a lot of belongings. Add to this John's stuff and the stuff from our three outbuildings and our barn. We had a giant task ahead of us. The end of the year was rapidly approaching, so time was of the essence.

John got a job hauling Christmas trees to California to supplement our income while he was out of work for the winter. During his first two trips there and back, I took pictures, wall hangings, and knick-knacks off the walls for packing. We planned to do the majority of sorting, saving, and scrapping during Christmas break, when I had time off from bus driving.

The first week of December, we started moving our necessities. By the end of the week, we were sleeping in our new home. I liked our new home. It was a big change from the farm, but we were happy to get away from the busy road that ran right in front of our property. Cars and trucks flew by our home day and night. We lost a lot of pets to the traffic. And, of course, there was the fatal accident that took my daughter's life.

There were times I wondered if I could part with my thoughts of Jessica on the farm. I felt I was leaving a piece of her there, but family and friends assured me that I wasn't. God gave us our memories to keep forever. Jessica would move right along with me.

We were in our new home for nearly two weeks, but we still hadn't moved half our belongings from the farm. Our new house was on a dead end street, quiet and peaceful. We were not used to having neighbors next door. I wondered many times if I could adjust to having people so close. After living on a farm for twenty-five years, I was used to doing what I wanted without having to worry about anyone watching me. But as we settled in, I noticed that the neighbors on each side of us kept to themselves and didn't appear to be watching us, which I feared they would. At that point, I knew I would adjust well.

On the morning of December 11, 2006, I left for work eager for the approaching Christmas break. Christmas was a time for much celebration with all our families' birthdays and anniversaries and listening to all the children on my bus chatter about what gifts they hoped to get for Christmas.

Late that afternoon I was finishing my last run of the day, which was my elementary children, kindergarten through fifth grade. I was driving down the road and noticed that one of my right front mirrors was hanging by a piece of wire. Fearing that I was going to lose my mirror, I radioed base to get permission to get off the bus and fix it at my next turnaround. I had only four kids left on my bus. I instructed them to behave as I took the keys out of the ignition and got out to fix the mirror. Another bus driver heard me call this request in and said she would meet me at the turnaround to trade buses, since hers was already empty. I agreed, and after getting permission from base, we met at the turnaround. Between the two of us, we repaired the mirror well enough for me to make it back to the bus barn and have the mechanic fix it completely. I told my fellow bus driver that I would continue on in my own bus and see her back at the bus barn in about fifteen minutes.

I drove back onto the main road, went a short distance, and dropped off three kids. I went about another quarter mile and dropped off my last student, telling him to have a nice evening and that I would see him the next day. As I put my foot to the gas peddle, I picked up speed and noticed a car in the other lane coming toward me with its blinker on. It appeared that the driver was waiting for me to pass before he turned into his driveway. I was closely watching his vehicle to make sure he didn't turn in front of me. All of a sudden a utility truck veered into my lane from behind the other car. A second went by, and I realized that this truck was not going to go back into his lane. A split second later I realized we were going to collide. I hung on for dear life.

I don't remember the initial crash, but I do recall hearing everything: the glass breaking, the tires squawking, the metal crunching, and the water from radiators hissing. After the impact, I fell back into my seat and wondered what just happened. The front windows were gone, and I noticed two men standing at the front right side of my bus, talking. I heard one of them say, "There is no use going over to the truck. The man inside is not going to make it. He is gurgling his last breath." I sensed how intense the collision had been at that moment. Panic quickly set in.

The impact of the collision caused the bus to land on the right side of the road, halfway in a driveway and halfway on the road. The utility truck completely spun around and ended up in the other lane, facing the direction it came from. It ended up beside me, to my left, but out of my sight. I had no idea what happened to the car that was waiting for me. I did not see it at all. Later, I found out that it sped ahead to avoid being rear-ended by the utility truck.

"Dear God, please be with me. Oh God, help me!" I prayed.

The emergency procedures I learned in my bus-driver training ran through my mind. I needed to radio my base to let them know I was in a wreck and that I needed help ASAP. As I went to reach for my radio, I felt tremendous pain in both of my legs. I grabbed the radio microphone, pushed the talk button, and realized it didn't work. Nothing worked!

I had my cell phone with me, and somehow I was able to find it. I called the office and said, "This is Lori, Route 8. I'm on Molalla Avenue, and I've been in a wreck. I need help ASAP."

Next, I called John, but I could not reach him. That morning he had gone to Redmond, Oregon, three hours away, to deliver a butchered pig to one of his best friends. Redmond was on the other side of the mountains. It was likely he had no reception on his cell phone.

I called my sister, but I couldn't get her either. I called my brother, Mike. He answered, and as soon as I heard his voice, I broke down and cried.

"Mike, this is Lori."

"What's the matter?"

"Mike, I've been in a horrible wreck, and I need you here."

I told him where I was, and he left to meet me.

I then tried calling my brother-in-law, Paul, who lived about one hundred yards from where the accident took place.

I knew he was close, and I wanted someone I knew by my side. He didn't answer, so I hung up.

I tried calling my husband one more time. This time he answered. He was coming through Sandy at that time, which was less than an hour away. He said he would be there as fast as he could. After I contacted the people I needed to, I sat and waited for someone to take care of me. As I was waiting, I realized that I wasn't sitting in my seat. I was on the floor, right next to the engine.

My bus had a flat front. The engine was beneath the floor, right next to the driver's seat. During the crash, the lid to the engine popped open. I was just inches from sitting on the hot motor. I used my arms to hold myself up so that I would not burn my behind. I had no clue what my injuries were.

"God, please be with me! I don't know what is going on!"

I felt God's Spirit with me. I remember talking to God, saying, "God, please take me if that is your choice. I am ready to be with Jessica and you." I was calm, yet a little scared, as I talked with God. If this was my time to go, I felt a peace about it.

"Do you need help?" asked the two men outside my bus.

"Yes!"

One of the gentlemen came over by the broken out windows and told me to open the front bus door, but it wouldn't open. I told him to crawl through the back of the bus and come up from behind to get to me. As he did this, I grew more anxious for help to arrive.

The man came up behind me and asked, "What can I do to help?"

"Pick me up, so I can shut the lid to the motor. I don't want to get burned."

As he lifted me from behind, I could feel the pain in my legs intensify. I panicked, not knowing what was wrong with me.

I asked the gentleman what his name was, but I can't remember what he said. I needed to talk to him to get my mind off my injuries and pass time until the emergency crew arrived. I asked him if he was from Molalla, and he said no. He was just passing through on a job. I never once saw this man's face.

He continued to hold me up so that I wouldn't get burned. He talked to me and comforted me. I have no idea who this man was or where he came from. I never saw him again. To this day, I call him my "angel in disguise."

Airborne

CHAPTER 3

It seemed like an eternity before the emergency people arrived on the scene. I heard the sound of sirens in the distance, and my heart started to pound in my chest. The police arrived first, and I could see them walking around the scene. Someone told me that the ambulance was there as well. Later, I found out that other emergency vehicles were called from a nearby town to help with road closures.

When the paramedics arrived, a fireman came to me and said that I would have to wait a little while longer for an ambulance from Canby (a nearby town) to show up. I was told that there was a passenger in the utility truck with life threatening injuries. Life Flight was called to fly him to a hospital in Portland. A few minutes later, the paramedics told me that another Life Flight was on the way to take me to a different hospital in Portland. When I heard this, I was relieved. This meant I would be at the hospital within minutes. This helped me relax a little bit.

Finally the ambulance from Canby arrived. Several paramedics came onto my bus. They asked me where I was hurting and looked for the best way to get me off the school bus. I kept thinking how lucky I was to have just dropped off my last student, just feet from where the accident happened.

If any children had been on the bus, there would have been many injuries or deaths.

I realized when the paramedics got on my bus that my angel in disguise was no longer there. To this day, I am still trying to find out who he was so that I can get in touch with him and thank him for the patience and the kindness he showed me.

The paramedics pulled me back away from the engine and lay me in the aisle. They brought a stretcher in and slid it under my body. It was not easy for them to lift me up inside the school bus with all the seats blocking the way. They lifted me up and told me to hold on to the sides of the stretcher. They had to carry me down the stairs of the bus. It was a ride I will not forget. I felt as though I was going to slip off the board, but I had a wonderful, experienced group of paramedics with me who did their jobs well.

Lori Loyer, one of my coworkers who also drove a school bus, and her husband Lonnie, who worked for the Molalla Fire Department, were at home when Lonnie received a call that a school bus had been in an accident. They hurried to their car, drove to the scene of the accident, and were at my side within minutes. When I saw them, some of my fear lifted. I knew they would tell me what was going on and what my injuries were. As soon as I saw Lori, I asked her what I looked like. I had no idea if my face was smashed, cut, or bleeding. I just knew my legs hurt badly. Lori looked at me and said I looked beautiful. If my nose were detached, she would have still told me that I looked beautiful, but her words were reassuring. She told me I had a cut on the left side of my face, but it wasn't bad.

While I was waiting in the ambulance for Life Flight to come, my brother, Mike, and his wife, Chris, arrived. I started to cry when I saw the fear in my brother's eyes. His look told me how horrific my accident really was. Mike took my hand, told me he loved me, and said that things were going to be just fine. People I knew were starting to come to the door of the ambulance: some coworkers, family, friends, and finally, John. When I saw my "Johnny Angel" my emotions swelled. I took comfort in the presence of the ones I loved. I also felt God's presence with us, which reminded me that my sweet Jessica was with me as well.

I asked John to call my boys to let them know what happened. He called Boone first. Boone had just moved to Boise, Idaho, and signed a two-year contract with a large company. He was coming home that particular weekend to attend his graduation ceremony from ITT Technical Institute. He was stuck in Idaho until Friday, a full four days after the accident. With a new job he had just started in Boise and not knowing anyone to confide in, the wait would be horrible for him, but I was glad he already had plans to come home.

John then called Brett at his work and told him I had been in an awful wreck. He told Brett which hospital they were taking me to, and instructed him to meet us there.

Meanwhile, the paramedics kept questioning me about my injuries, where and how much I hurt. After I described my pains, they told me they were going to cut my clothes off to check for internal injuries. Sure enough, they cut off all my clothes. Once they finished checking my body for injuries, they covered me with blankets to keep me warm. My legs were in massive pain, and I did not want anyone to touch them or move them. My chest was also hurting. It scared me to think of what was wrong with it.

Finally, I heard the sound of a helicopter approaching. The helicopter landed in a field right across the street from my brother-in-law's house. The paramedics opened the back doors of the ambulance and told me exactly what was going to happen. It was raining as they went to transport me, so they covered me well with blankets and held an umbrella over my head to keep me as dry as possible.

I felt a peace come over me. Within minutes I would be at the hospital in Portland, and I would be getting the treatment I needed for my injuries. They lifted me into the open side of the helicopter and put me into place for the ride ahead.

I was not at all scared of the ride. I prayed the whole time, asking God for His peace and to prepare my doctors ahead of time to take care of me.

I knew from the experience of Boone's accident that I would be by myself at the hospital for about an hour before my family would arrive. When we got to the hospital, the landing was a little rough, but I was relieved to be there.

The trauma team met us at the landing pad and unloaded me from the helicopter. They rolled me into the trauma center, telling me there would be a lot of doctors and nurses in the room at one time. I was told the reason for so many people being there was that they each had a specific job to do on different parts of my body.

I answered all their questions, and I begged them not to work on my legs because they were massively in pain. My chest was still hurting, and my head was hurting as well.

I have no idea how long I was in the trauma center before they wheeled me to another room. All I know it that I was alone for quite some time. I cried as thoughts of the collision came to my mind. I could not get the pictures and the sounds out of my head. I kept praying to God to help me through this.

Once my family started coming through the doors, I lost it. Tears flowed from my eyes. I was relieved that the people I loved more than anything on earth were finally with me.

I asked my husband several times if the man driving the truck was okay. He kept avoiding the question, so I pushed for an answer. He told me the man died at the scene. My heart was jolted by the news. I trembled at the recollection of the accident. I could still see the truck coming at me in my lane. There was nothing, nothing at all that I could have done to stop it.

When Brett finally arrived from work, I sobbed and held my hand out for him to take as tragedies of old passed through my mind. I held his hand and kept him near me for my own comfort.

Not much later, a nurse came in and told me that I was being assigned a private room. When they wheeled me into my new room around seven o'clock that night, it was full of family and friends, with more waiting in the hall outside. Each of them wanted to hold my hand and comfort me. A nurse took John aside and asked if he could politely ask them to leave so that I could rest. John did as he was instructed. He promised everyone that he would keep them informed of any changes.

Soon, everyone was gone except John. He told me to try to rest as he settled into a recliner. This would become his bed for the next few days.

My bus at the scene of the accident

A Slow Process

CHAPTER 4

When I woke up the next morning, the aches and pains of the crash were very real to me. It made me cry to move just a couple inches in my bed. Breakfast was at hand, but I was told that I wouldn't get any because I might be going into surgery that day.

The doctors came in one by one, poking, prodding, and explaining to John and me what my injuries consisted of. When I was in the trauma center the night before, they ordered X-rays, CT scans, and other tests to determine if I had any internal injuries.

The knee doctor came to visit and explained that there was severe trauma to my left knee, but he couldn't tell much from the X-rays. He ordered an MRI to determine if I would need surgery. He said my right knee looked fine; it was just badly bruised and punctured from the impact. While I waited for my MRI to be taken, I still wasn't allowed to eat.

The trauma doctor came in and informed me that the reason my chest hurt was because I hit the steering wheel at full force. I later found out I had hit it so hard with my chest that I bent it. My sternum was severely bruised, but no bones were broken in that area, not even a single rib. I just had very sore muscles that would take time to heal.

After talking with the doctors that morning, I kept going over the crash in my mind. I still cried at times, thinking of the wreck and wondering *why?* I prayed God would help me with my pain and to push past the thoughts that consumed me. I prayed He would help me get through one day at a time. I knew it was going to be a long healing process.

John and I waited all day for the MRI to be taken. Finally, when the nurse took me to get the MRI, they immobilized my knee. I begged them to be careful when they moved me. They lifted me onto the table and told me to lie completely still, so I used this time for prayer. I prayed to God to help the technicians get the best pictures they needed to help fix my knee and get on with my healing process. When they were finished, they laid me back on my bed in my private room and gave me more medication.

The evening hours were upon us, so John went down to the cafeteria to get a bite to eat while I slept. My family came to visit me. Brett came in straight after work. Seeing the love and concern coming through his eyes made me feel good. I knew I was loved, and the more love I saw, the better I felt. John updated everyone who came to visit about what the doctors said that day and what tests we were waiting for.

As the second evening was ending, I was still not allowed to eat. No one was sure if I would need surgery. All I was allowed to do was suck on some ice chips to wet my dry mouth.

As I lay in bed that night, I thought of how crazy things can get in life. I wondered about people who do not have God in their lives. How do they cope without having anything to lean on? I knew I could count on Christ, and I knew He had a plan for me. I just didn't know at the time what it was.

When morning came, my husband and I talked about the uncomfortable sleep we experienced. I was getting quite stiff in many areas, and my chest and legs were in massive pain. I was still not allowed to eat.

John mentioned that he really wanted to drive home, take a shower, check on our dogs, get the mail, and do some things that hadn't been done for three days. I told him to go ahead. I really wanted to sleep, and we weren't sure when the doctor would be in to see me.

After John left for home, I spent time alone with my Lord. I kept telling God that I was so very thankful that He spared me, unlike the man who ran into my bus. I had to wonder what the man was doing, why he didn't see a big yellow bus driving down the road. What could have been so important that he couldn't focus on his driving? I concluded that I might never know the answers to my questions, so I shut my eyes and went to sleep.

I woke up to see a coworker, Judy, and my boss standing in my room. Judy told me that on the day of the accident she heard over the radio that a bus had been involved in a wreck. She had frantically been calling me on the radio, trying to get me to respond. I began to cry when Judy told me that all the bus drivers gave me their prayers and support. I told my boss that I really did not want to drive a flat nose bus any longer. There was nothing in front to protect me from the impact. "We'll work something out," she said. "For now, concentrate on your healing."

Sometime around noon, the knee doctor came. After examining the MRI, he said surgery should be done as soon as possible. My kneecap had been crushed, and he wouldn't know the extent of the damage until he got inside the knee to examine it further. I signed consent forms and agreed to enter surgery within the hour.

A few minutes later, the nurses came in and started preparing me for surgery, scrubbing the damaged area, shaving my knee stubble as best they could without hurting me, and giving me medication to start the process of putting me to sleep. The anesthesiologist came into my room and informed me of all that was about to take place.

"Have you eaten anything?" he asked.
I laughed!

***

When I awoke after surgery, I was back in my own room. The first face I saw was my sweet Johnny Angel. I wiggled a little bit, and I felt agonizing pain in my leg. I looked under the covers to see what had been done to me, but my knee was all wrapped up, making it appear twice its normal size.

The rest of the day, I drifted in and out of consciousness. Toward evening, a sense of reality returned and my stomach roared with hunger. I told my nurse I really needed something to eat. I wasn't given that much, but once I swallowed some food, I felt a calm settle in my stomach.

The nurses changed shifts two or three times per day. Some nurses had twelve-hour shifts, some eight-hour shifts. During one of the shifts that carried over into the wee hours of the morning, a nurse came into my room and must have thought I was asleep. I could hear her speaking to God: "Dear Jesus, bless her and keep her safe," and "Jesus, sweet Jesus, bless her and comfort her." At first I thought I was dreaming, until I talked back to her. She was a comfort to my soul. She always talked about Jesus and God. She told me that she was there to take care of me, just as Jesus took care of His disciples. I looked forward to my midnight rests. I knew God's nurse would be there to watch over me.

The day after surgery, I looked in a mirror and realized that the person staring back at me needed help. I asked John for my hairbrush, a little blush, and a little light colored lipstick. After pampering myself, John said that I looked like I finally had some color.

My back itched as I brushed my hair. Something was irritating my skin. John had me lean forward so that he could take a look. He discovered that my back was full of little pieces of windshield glass. My head was also full of tiny slivers of glass. My whole bed was infested with it! John called the nurse to have someone come in and change my sheets and shampoo my hair. Unfortunately, I couldn't get my hair washed for another day. Volunteers provided this service for the hospital.

After my bedding was changed, I was given a full breakfast, something I had not had in three days. Next a physical therapist came to my room and told me she was going to get me out of bed and school me on how I would get around for the next few months. I wasn't anticipating this moment at all. My pain was intense, and I knew getting out of bed was going to hurt. I warned the nurse I was a fainter. She acknowledged me, but was persistent about getting me up.

The therapist brought in a huge leg brace that encased my leg from the top of my thigh to the bottom of my ankle. It had Velcro straps all the way down it. The doctor left instructions after my surgery that I was not to bend my knee or put any weight on it at all.

The therapist adjusted the brace so that I could not bend my knee at all. Zero degrees. This black leg brace would be my worst enemy and my closest companion throughout my recovery. I grew to hate the sound of Velcro.

When the therapist told me to sit up and swing my legs over the edge of the bed, the blood rushed to my injury. I once again warned the therapist that I was a fainter. She told me to slow down. It took several minutes before I could actually sit up on the edge of my bed with my feet touching the floor. I had not touched the floor in three days, but I was ready to tackle something new.

My goal was to stand up on crutches, walk three feet to the reclining chair, and sit in the chair for a while. As I leaned on the crutches, all my weight was in my arms. "One, two, three" and up I stood. Again, all the blood rushed to my left knee. I reached the recliner before dizziness overcame me. I flopped into the chair, and when my senses returned,

I saw a big smile come across everyone's faces. The feeling of accomplishment overwhelmed me and tears came to my eyes, but the tears quickly turned to fears. I wasn't sure if I would ever walk normal again.

I sat in my chair all morning. It felt good to be out of my bed. While I was still in the chair, the knee doctor came to see how things were going. He was astonished at how well I was doing. He commented on my looks (the brightness from blush and lip stick) and on the change in my demeanor. He said that when he got inside the knee, he found that my kneecap was fractured into pieces. He said that he had drilled little holes into those pieces, used some fine thread to go through those holes, then he pulled them all together like a fish net and secured them into place. I also had some damaged ligaments and tendons that didn't show up in the MRI, but he had fixed them all. I was told that I could not, under any circumstances, put any weight on my left leg. I must allow the ligaments and tendons to heal for at least four to six weeks. I had an appointment to go back to his office in two weeks to be examined and receive new instructions.

The trauma doctor came to my room next. He explained to me that when I arrived, my body had been X-rayed and scanned for unseen injuries. When the test results came back, they discovered I had a cyst on my kidney, a cyst on my liver, and a small nodule on my lung. As the doctor spoke, all that registered was "a small nodule on my lung." He said he wasn't overly concerned about the cysts on my kidney and liver, but he was a little concerned about the nodule on my lung. He said I needed to make an appointment with a lung doctor within the next six months to make sure the nodule hadn't grown. My cysts should be checked within three months to make sure they hadn't grown as well. He gave me the names of specialists to call when I got out of the hospital.

When Friday came, John went to the airport to pick up Boone. His graduation was taking place that evening. When Boone came walking through the door of my room, I lost it.

"Hi mom!"

"Hello Boone. I am so glad you are here finally."

"You are going to be okay mom. We will get through this, all of us."

As we hugged, I thought of all the things we endured together: his accident, Jessica's death, and now this accident that could have easily taken my life. I have a very strong bond with my sons because of the sufferings we endured.

I could tell by Boone's emotional responses that he felt relieved to be home, to be able to communicate with me instead of getting phone calls from family members. Boone needed to see for himself that I was going to be okay. Living away from home during emergency situations such as this would be hard for him. I encouraged him to lean on Jesus for comfort and strength and reminded him that we were just a phone call away.

Time passed quickly. It was soon time for John to take Boone home to prepare for his ceremony. I knew I wouldn't see my sons, John, or any family that evening. They would all be attending the graduation. I asked everyone to take lots of pictures for me. I cried again because I wanted to be there at the ceremony.

The next morning, the doctors would visit me and decide if I could be released from the hospital. I couldn't wait for morning to come. I was ready to go home.

Going Home

CHAPTER 5

Morning arrived. After I ate breakfast, I had to use the restroom. This was something I had to do without help if I wanted to prove I was ready to go home. I was determined to take on this task and convince the doctors to let me go. Mission accomplished!

One by one, the doctors came in and agreed to release me from the hospital.

When the paperwork was completed, the nurse came in with a wheelchair for my departure. To the end of the hall and down the elevator I went with a wagon full of flowers, cards, and gifts trailing behind me. John went to get the pickup, and once I was in it, I waived good-bye to the nurse. Off to our house we went.

We hadn't gone far when I felt overwhelmed by the events that had taken place in the last several days. Riding down the road gave me a sense of freedom from the accident, but I wondered how many more bad events I would endure. Would this be the last one? Once again, I thanked God for His protection during the accident.

As we were nearing our home, we turned onto the road where my accident occurred. John asked me if it would bother me to drive through that area, and I said no, I actually wanted to check out the scene where it happened. When we approached the scene, we slowed down. I looked at where my bus ended up. Broken glass and skid marks were still on the road. I got chills through my body as memories of the crash played in my mind. Within seconds, we were past the scene and closer to home.

I could not wait to get inside my new house and rest in peace and quiet. As I hobbled through the front door, our dogs greeted me with happy faces, wagging tails, and wet kisses. They missed me as much as I missed them. I hobbled over to my recliner and plopped down into the soft cushiony seat. This was my new bed for the next few months.

The next couple of days, I received a lot of company, mostly people who didn't want to come to the hospital for fear of bothering me. Once I was at home, I was never alone.

Soon after I was home, John's daughter Megan, her husband Jack and our grand-daughter Kylie came by for a visit. For some reason I decided to check my wound. As I took off my brace and bandages, my two-year-old grand-daughter, Kylie Mae, watched me. When I got to the end of the ace bandages, I pulled off the piece of gauze that sat on my wound. Kylie's facial expression went from excited to frightened. I thought she was going to cry. We were both shocked by the severity of what the doctor had done. My knee was red and severely swollen, making it hard to tell where my knee stopped and my thigh began. The stitches covered the whole knee area. They looked liked railroad tracks.

My mom brought over my late grandmother's walker as an option instead of crutches. I used it to steady myself as I stood to get out of my chair. Each time I got up, the blood rushed down my leg into the wounded area. It throbbed and ached with such force that it made me cry.

My mom came by daily to be my nurse as John moved the rest of our stuff over from the farm. This is when we realized how fortunate we were that the buyers of our farm gave us so much time to move.

During this time, my dad was suffering from Parkinson's Disease. He was developing some minor stages of dementia as well. My father had been the pillar of our family. Dad was a very successful business man who logged for several years. He made quite a name for himself in Oregon when he became president of the Oregon Loggers Association. He was very involved as a deacon in our church. He generously helped others, knowing God had blessed him financially for this very purpose. During my recovery, Dad felt most comfortable in his own house. Although my mom came daily to help me, I saw little of my dad.

Brett's twenty-first birthday was approaching. We planned for months to take Brett to dinner on his birthday, December 23. I was determined to keep my word, but I wanted to go somewhere close to home. John rented me a wheelchair. Not only did it make it easier to move me, it was the only way I could sit at a table. It felt good to be out, but within minutes of getting settled at our table, I realized I might have made a mistake. I started feeling faint, tired, and generally unwell. We ordered our food, and after a quick meal, I wanted to go home. I was exhausted by the time I sat back down in my recliner, but I felt satisfied. The birthday dinner was accomplished.

The rest of the holiday season — Christmas Eve, Christmas Day, New Years Eve (our anniversary) and New Years Day — was spent mostly with our family. These days were emotional for me. I thought of how precious each day was and how fortunate it was to me to be alive and celebrating the birth of our Lord Jesus Christ. Throughout the season I concentrated on my past, the things that I had endured, and what I could do to face the future. I thought about this a lot, and I concluded that I needed to be more resolute in my stance for Christ, not to be afraid that I would be ridiculed or taunted if I spoke out about God. I had every reason to spread the gospel of our Lord to family and friends. I decided I wanted to share more of my faith with others. I had many friends whom I decided I was going to talk to about Christ and what He did for me. I wanted to shout the love of God to everyone!

By the time the holidays were over, John finished moving all our stuff from the farm. We were completely moved into our new home.

Before I knew it, I was on my way back to the doctor's for follow-up visits. We went to the trauma center first, and the doctor said he was releasing me from his services.

Next we went to the knee doctor, where he took X-rays and examined my knee. My X-rays looked good, the knee cap was in its proper place, and all the pieces he threaded together appeared to be healing. The doctor proceeded to take out my stitches, which had been in my knee for almost three weeks. As you can imagine, they were quite embedded in my skin. As they pulled out one stitch at a time, it was agonizing.

After all the stitches were taken out, the doctor told me the healing was going as it should, it would just take time. He adjusted my brace so I could bend my knee a few degrees, but I was still advised not to put any bearing weight on my foot. I could touch my toes to the ground, but I was not to put any weight into my step. He ordered me to attend physical therapy. I was to go two or three times per week for three months before he would even consider releasing me to go back to work.

I was leery of attending my first physical therapy session, worried I would be brutally abused and have to deal with a lot of pain. The therapist followed the doctor's instructions, and to my surprise, there was little pain. The therapist simply lifted my leg, which I was not able to do on my own, and massaged my muscles.

When my next doctor's appointment came, there were more X-rays to be taken. When the X-rays were over, the doctor asked me to pick my leg up off the table. I could not do it. I was astounded that I simply could not lift my leg off the table. I wondered what was wrong with me, if I was going to be able to ever use my leg again. He assured me this was normal. My muscles and tissue had not been used for a very long time. The doctor wrote specific instructions for the therapists to begin some leg strengthening exercises and told me to start putting weight into my walk. I was instructed to do no work for another eight weeks, just to keep resting and going to physical therapy.

There were many times I thought about the bad things that had happened to me. I wondered if I had done something wrong in my life to endure such trials. Through these tough and trying times I always looked to God for answers. God was always there, and I knew He was not going to leave me at any time. Although I might not have been very happy during these events, I felt God's presence in all these accidents. I started to feel as though I should share my stories and to give hope to others who are hurting. After sharing these feelings with my two sons, they encouraged me that I should continue to write about my accidents and how God had worked in my life. I needed to share with others who were hurting and give them hope that God will comfort them if they put their fears and misfortunes into His hands.

I often thought of the passenger who survived in the truck that hit me. He had to be grieving the loss of his friend as he dealt with his own injuries. I found out from Cheryl, a friend of mine, that the utility truck that hit me belonged to a friend of hers. The driver and the passenger, Donny, were on their way to Cheryl's house when we collided. I called Cheryl several times to find out how Donny was. He was still in the hospital three months after the accident. During that time, the doctors had to amputate his leg because of an infection that would not heal properly. Once the amputation was completed, he was transported to a nursing home in my hometown to learn how to live life without his leg.

One day as I was driving to the grocery store, I passed by Donny's nursing home. For some reason, I decided it was time to meet him and see how he was doing. I wasn't sure how he would respond to me, but this was something that I needed to do to gain some closure on the situation. Donny was just returning from a doctor's visit when I walked up the sidewalk to go inside. I wasn't sure if the man I saw was the right man or not, but he did have only one leg. As I approached him I asked, "Are you Donny?"

"Yes I am."

"I'm Lori Koos, the person who was driving the school bus in our accident."

I could tell that he needed a hug, but as I walked toward him, I could see he was in pain. I refrained from hugging him, giving him a long, strong handshake instead. We sat and talked for some time. I could tell that his memory was not clear; he didn't really remember much about the accident. He sounded quite bitter about being messed up. I told him that he needed to give his worries to God. He offered little response to my suggestion.

I left the nursing home feeling satisfied that I met the only other survivor of my accident, but my heart ached for him. He was in pain still, carrying all his aggressions on his shoulders. I realized that I can't change people's minds about my Lord, but I can still talk to them about Him.

I also wondered if I would be able to drive a school bus again. People asked me about it all the time. At some point, I would have to make a decision about returning to work. I decided to talk to a counselor and discuss my feelings and options.

I couldn't remember parts of my accident. My counselor said that when a traumatic accident happens, many times they happen so quickly that our brain can't register all the sensory input, so it will bypass the processing stage. Eventually, the memories will start to surface and work their way to the forefront of the mind. This is exactly what happened. As time passed, I started to remember things that were locked in my mind. Many people used to ask me what it was like to see the truck coming down my lane, knowing it was going to hit my bus. They asked if I had seen the people in it. I can't really say that I saw the people, but there were times when I saw in flash-like visions a face with big eyes and a mouth opened in shock. When I see this vision, I have no idea if this is really what I saw.

* * *

Weeks passed by, and I started putting pressure on my leg. I finally gave up the walker and the wheelchair, but not the crutches. My legs still ached, but I continued working on them through therapy.

I started to miss the students that rode my bus. Several of them had called, sent cards and gifts, and even come to my house to visit me. It was these times when I was reminded of why I chose to drive a school bus. I loved the kids!

One day, about three months after my accident, being massively bored, I told my mom I wanted to go to the elementary school and stand by my bus when the kids were let out of school. My mom took me to school, and I asked the principal for permission to see my kids. Of course he agreed. When I made it to my bus, the driver taking my place was happy to see me. She knew how my kids were going to react when they saw me. One by one, the classes were let out. As the kids came closer to the bus, they realized who I was. I gave each child a big hug. Tears and hellos were exchanged.

I realized how much the children missed me. This filled my heart with joy.

After the children were loaded on the bus, I scooted back on the sidewalk, waved to them, and blew them kisses until my bus was out of sight. I left Mulino Elementary School that day with a big smile on my face. I also left with doubts in my mind. I wasn't sure if I still wanted to, or even if I could, drive a school bus again. I had a lot of thinking to do, and only a couple months left to make up my mind. Regardless, it was good medicine for me to see the kids. I missed them very much.

Behind the Wheel Again

CHAPTER 6

Eight weeks went by, and it was time once again to see my doctor. He took more X-rays to compare to my last X-rays. Things were healing well. The strength in my leg was returning. I could actually lift my leg off the table this time. I was advised to start putting full weight into my walk while continuing to use my leg brace. The doctor increased the mobility in the brace to where I could bend my knee during each step. At this time he released me to start driving a bus, but with limitation. Despite the release, my employers would not let me drive the bus until all the restrictions were lifted. However, I was able to drive my own car, which gave me some needed independence.

Since I was unable to drive a school bus, my days were used for whatever my boss thought I could do under my restrictions. I filed papers, answered phones, and did whatever I was told to do. I was getting back into the groove of things—this time with a different outlook on life. I felt refreshed. I had a sense that waking up each morning would bring me a happy desire to be thankful for everything: life, work, family, friends, and God. I was never a very patient person, but because I lived in my recliner for several months, I learned to take things as they came. When I wanted something that was out of my reach, I had to wait. At some point, someone would walk my way and ask if there was anything they could help me with.

In May, the doctor told me that there was no reason why I shouldn't be able to drive bus. He lifted all of my restrictions and limitations. The doctor signed my paperwork and told me to come back in August for the final inspection of my leg. At that time he would take measurements of my leg and record any permanent disabilities. I left the office that day not having to wear my brace any longer. No more would I endure the daily sound of Velcro straps being ripped apart. I walked out of the office with my brace in hand and dumped it in the first trashcan I found.

I hoped to drive my school bus again within the next couple days. School would be out for summer vacation in one more month. I wanted to get behind the wheel that last month to squish the fears I had of driving through the accident area. I took all the paperwork to my boss and told her I was released to drive. First, she told me, I had to take a couple tests to make sure I was still capable.

My boss rode with me on a quick run down the road. She wanted to make sure I was okay with driving again. Once in my assigned bus (not a flat-nose one any longer), I sat down in my seat, fastened my seat belt, and beamed to know that I was defeating my fears. My boss made me drive through the area where my accident took place, and I did so with ease.

After my trial run, I was released to drive solo once again. I was able to start the second leg of my morning route, picking up my kindergarten through fifth graders. I anticipated their surprise at seeing me. I couldn't wait to see their faces.

As I rolled up to each stop, each child looked to see what driver they had for that day. The kids had so many different substitute drivers that they never knew whom they were going to get. As I turned my flashers on and rolled to a complete stop, each kid realized it was me. Every single one of them got a great big "Oh!" smile on their faces, hugged me, and welcomed me back. It brought tears to my eyes.

It was great to have my grandson's back on my "shuttle" bus, a bus that took students from the middle school to the high school to catch the buses that took them home. When my grandson's started middle school, they would ride my bus and sit behind me to chat. I missed them terribly when I was recovering. To be able to see them daily again was a delight for me.

It was such a good feeling being back at work. My coworkers were so supportive of me. Many asked me why I came back. When they did, I would look at them and say, "I drive because I love kids. The same reason you drive." I knew what they were thinking. Many told me that it takes a strong person to get back on that bus and drive again. But I did, and it felt great.

After driving for a month, my eyes were set on the last day of school, June 6, 2007. I looked forward to finally resting, relaxing, and concentrating on my healing. The doctor told me that swimming and bicycling were the best exercises for me. I intended to do a lot of both that summer.

On the last day of school, bus drivers, students, and teachers' spirits were high, anticipating the beginning of summer vacation. As my bus passed by the teachers all lined up on the sidewalk, I allowed the kids to roll down their windows to yell and wave as we pulled out of the school for the last time. Dropping each kid off at their locations, I told each one of them to have a wonderful summer and that I would see them next year. The kids had been asking me all along if I was going to be coming back that next year. I told them most likely I was. After my last student was dropped off, I parked my bus, swept it, turned in my paperwork, cleaned out my locker, and turned in the keys.

At the end of the day, our depot had a luncheon put on by our management. It was nice to sit, relax, eat and talk to my fellow drivers. We chatted about our plans for the summer and the relaxation that goes along with having our summers off.

As I was walking to my car the last thing I remember saying as I left was, "Wow, what a ride it was!"

I am Restored

CHAPTER 7

I have grown spiritually because of my accident. I am thankful to God for sparing my life. I could have died in my bus, but I was spared! I could have had a leg amputated, but I was spared! I could have lost students in the accident, but they were spared! My injuries were not life threatening, even though my recovery was long. God more than proved His love for me.

I remember waiting for the ambulance to come, telling God I was ready to go be with Him. I truly was. I remember thinking about my Jessica with Jesus at that particular moment. That is right where I wanted to be. I was ready, but God wasn't ready for me.

My perspective on life is different now. I know that God is good and wants the best for everyone, but I also know that not everyone knows my God. I'm compelled to share my faith more and not worry if I offend someone. Others need to be convicted of what the Bible says.

The best way I know to tell others of the love of Jesus is to do what I am doing right now, sharing my story about how He brought me through these three tragic events. There are times when I hear friends complaining about trivial things, things that are really nothing to worry about. They let these things consume so much of their energy. It frustrates me to see that energy go to waste. During those times, I try to say something positive to them that will help them look at their problems in a different perspective, to make them understand there are people out there who have much larger problems than theirs. Many times it doesn't work. But that's not the issue. It's my job to show compassion and also not to focus on myself, but to help others in times of need.

I can't say that any one accident out of the three that impacted me was worse than the others. They all hurt. With the loss of my daughter, I had thoughts that I would never be able to live a happy life again. When I ran over my own son, I thought I would never be able to recover from the guilt. But, I routinely woke up to another sunrise on the horizon, another set of the minutes and hours ticking by. I would go about my day and another sunset would occur, another moonrise would fill the night sky. I call it life. And what a good life it is! And what a good life it can be if you have Jesus in it. I wonder how anyone could get through a tragedy without looking to Jesus for strength. God tells us that He will carry our load for us.

> *No temptation has seized you except what is common to man. And God is faithful; he will not let you be tempted beyond what you can bear. But when you are tempted, he will also provide a way out so that you can stand up under it. (1 Corinthians 10:13)*

When life puts a fork in the road, we can choose a dead end path, be miserable, blame others for our mishaps, and continue to live in misery and bring others down with us. Or we can choose to turn away from that dead end road and take a road that leads to life. I remember making that choice. I remember wanting to end my life until God opened my eyes to show me that I had two beautiful boys that needed their mother. When He did, I completely changed roads without reservations. I asked God for His guidance. I could not walk that road alone.

I am not a perfect example of a God-fearing Christian, but I do know what God expects of me. I know where I should be in my Christian life, and it will probably take the rest of my life on earth to even come close to being what I would like to be. But through it all, I know God's love will never fail me.

For I am convinced that neither death nor life, neither angels nor demons, neither the present nor the future, nor any powers, neither height nor depth, nor anything else in all creation, will be able to separate us from the love of God that is in Christ Jesus our Lord. (Romans 8:38 & 39)

I am who I am. I am me! I accept the things that have happened in my life, and I am still dealing with them. I can't change what happened. I can't say that I have never felt like I needed sympathy, because I have. I can't say that I haven't told my story and expected a "you poor lady" reaction, because I have. But God has allowed me to tell my story and then tell it again. He knows someone will see that I am just an ordinary person who has acknowledged Him on my journey of life.

I acknowledge Jesus Christ in my life, and I know what the Holy Bible says is the truth. That truth tells me that people need to accept Jesus Christ into their lives and acknowledge Him as their Lord and Savior in order to spend eternity in heaven with Him.

If you haven't, you should read the poem "Footprints." It tells of an individual walking along the beach, but two sets of footprints are in the sand: one is the person's and one is God's. All of a sudden, only one set of footprints remains, making it appear that God abandoned His child. But it was just the opposite. God picked up the weary soul and carried him. God never leaves us. I've learned that lesson well.

Use your time well, and remember to tell your family and friends how much they mean to you. Your loved ones can never be told enough how much you love them. You never know when a tragic, life-altering situation will tear you apart.

I pray that peace will be with you if you are seeking the Lord Jesus Christ in your life, and I pray you will search the Bible for answers to your pain.

One of my favorite verses I find comfort in during my time of need is this:

> *"Brothers, I do not consider myself yet to have taken hold of it. But one thing I do: Forgetting what is behind and straining toward what is ahead, I press on toward the goal to win the prize for which God has called me heavenward in Christ Jesus."*
> *(Philippians 3:13-14)*

> *In this you greatly rejoice, though now for a little while you may have had to suffer grief in all kinds of trials. These have come so that your faith—of greater worth than gold, which perishes even though refined by fire—may be proved genuine and may result in praise, glory and honor when Jesus Christ is revealed. Though you have not seen him, you love him; and even though you do not see him now, you believe in him and are filled with an inexpressible and glorious joy, for you are receiving the goal of your faith, the salvation of your souls.*
> *(1 Peter 1:6–9)*

Through each incident I went through, I was left feeling helpless and useless. I was not able to fix the situation. In response to those helpless feelings, I learned to gain strength and to stand up for what I believe in. I learned to listen more closely to what people had to say. I grew more conscious of my environment, and I took the time to see God's work in nature. I focused on turning my negative feelings into something that I had control over. This process has made me the strong person I am today. Out of my negatives I developed my positives, and I can happily cope with life now.

When bad things happen to people, the most common questions I hear are "Why God? Why me?" I have heard very spiritual people ask these questions. As I look back, I never, ever expected something to go so wrong that it would shake my foundation of life. God loves us so much; He doesn't want bad things to happen either. He wants to comfort us. Don't blame God for bad events; blame the evil one, Satan, for causing such uproar. God is the only one to heal our souls, and He wants us to seek Him for assurance and trust.

Praise be to the God and Father of our Lord Jesus Christ, the Father of compassion and the God of all comfort, who comforts us in all our troubles, so that we can comfort those in any trouble with the comfort we ourselves have received from God. (II Corinthians 1:3 & 4)

I went to my follow-up appointments regarding the cysts the doctors found on my liver and kidney. I was informed that neither had grown and was told that I shouldn't be worried about them growing in the future. I did however go to the "lung" doctor and had two more sets of x-rays taken. Neither of them showed any signs of growth as well. I was advised that I could let it go and not be bothered by it any longer, or I could wait two more years and have one more check up to make sure it has not grown. I opted for waiting two more years and have one more x-ray taken. That will be in the near future.

To this day I sometimes put up that wall in my head when I think about past events. When times get hectic and I feel as though I need a break from the monotonous world, I remember some of my tougher times and how I managed to make it through. Then, the hectic things don't seem hectic any longer.

When I first wrote Boone's story, he was a freshman in high school. I had written notes all during his accident and thereafter. Boone is now twenty-five years old. He received a bachelor's degree with honors, has a great job, and is serving the Lord with all his heart.

Brett is twenty-two years old. He wasn't born yet when we encountered Boone's accident, and he was only three years old when Jessica died. Brett has lived with family and friends, talking continuous about his sister and how she was a great example of what Christ would like us all to be. Brett has a close resemblance of his sister, without the red hair. He has developed a relationship connecting him to his sister through these circumstances.

Both of my boys love life and have been blessed with the gift of compassion. They care about people and hurt when others hurt. They acknowledge God and know they need Him in their lives.

Jessica would be twenty-eight years old now if she were alive. I wonder many times what she would look like, if she'd be married with children, and what sort of career she would have chosen. Every once in a while I see her old friends that are all grown up and married. I wonder if they would still be friends with her. One thing I do know, Jessica would still be praising God if she were here today.

"Hi Mom"

I'm doing fine
My hair's still red, my eyes still shine,
And it stays curly all of the time.
I love you Mom, I know you love me.
Life up here is all God says it will be.
No pain, no worry, just peace of mind.
It won't be long before it's your time.
I talk to Jesus to be kind to you, to help with
The things you must be going through.
I know you're sad and you miss me,
But once you get here you'll understand what happened
was a blessing to me.
My life up here is so great.
You will be coming, and I just can't wait!
I will have everything ready for you,

Then eternity will be ours.
When I think of that day, I give out a cheer!
Keep looking to God for the help you need,
It won't be that long you will see....
So give my love to the boys and to Dad.
Merry Christmas! Happy birthday, too!
I will keep talking to Jesus for you!
Love Jessi

(By Randy Noble, Jessica's father, 1989)

ACKNOWLEDGEMENT

I would like to thank my family and friends who have inspired me to finish this book that I started years ago. At that time, I had only penciled my thoughts during Boone's accident. Through counseling I was advised to continue with my writing. It was good therapy for me. I quit writing after Jessica's accident because it was too painful to write about my daughter who passed away. It wasn't until my bus accident, when all these emotions came flooding from within, that I picked up the pen and wrote again.

To Boone and Brett, I love you both. You are my world, and after all these trying and horrible times, we can sing songs to Jesus again. There were many times I wasn't sure if I could keep on going, but it was the two of you who brought me through my toughest times in life. I regret having to put you both through some tough periods growing up. Now that you both are older, I think you can understand why I was so persistent on always wanting to know where you were going, who you were going with, and the twenty questions I would always ask before you walked out the door. You two are always my shining stars, and we know that one day we will be with Jessica again. Remember the Diana Ross song, "Someday We'll Be Together."

To my husband, John, I love you more than you will ever know. You have been very supportive of me as I wrote this book. I'm sorry that it has consumed so much of my time. But you know it was something I needed to do, and here it is! All the hours you spent editing these pages and giving your input has made this book read the way it was intended. Thank you so very much. You have been so good to my boys, and they love you just as much in return.

I would also like to thank Vinnie Kinsella, Senior Editor at Declaration Editing, for all your help making this story read the way it should. I could not have done this without your expertise in editing. It was a blessing on top of everything else to find out you were a believer in Christ, something that I had been praying for. Your wisdom helped make my story come alive in areas I was not sure about.

Life is good!

If you would like to know more about how to deal with grief, or want to know more about seeking Jesus Christ as your Savior, please send me an email. I would love to hear from you.

grieftogracebook@molalla.net

www.grieftogracebook.com

Printed in the United States
215448BV00001B/2/P

9 781607 914990